HOW THE
PERSHORE PLUM
WON THE
GREAT WAR

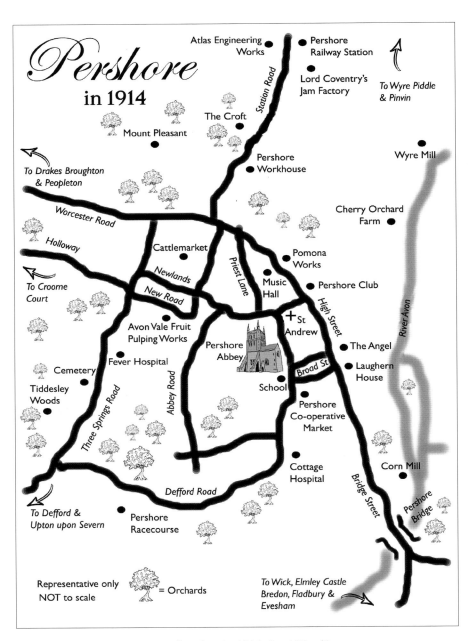

Map of Pershore in 1914. (Jenni Waugh)

HOW THE PERSHORE PLUM WON THE GREAT WAR

EDITED BY MAGGIE ANDREWS & JENNI WAUGH

The History Press

To our mothers,
grandmothers and the
women who brought
them up.

First published 2016

The History Press
The Mill, Brimscombe Port
Stroud, Gloucestershire, GL5 2QG
www.thehistorypress.co.uk

British Library Cataloguing in Publication Data.
A catalogue record for this book is available from the British Library.

ISBN 978 0 7509 6516 3

Typesetting and origination by The History Press
Printed in Malta, by Melita Press.

CONTENTS

໑๐ ๑๐

	About the Editors	6
	Acknowledgements	7
	Introduction	9
1	War Comes to Pershore	19
	Emily Linney and University of Worcester History Students	
2	Growing Food in the Market Gardens and Farms of Pershore	30
	Pershore Heritage and History Society and University of Worcester History Students	
3	Who is Bringing in the Harvest?	43
	Pershore Heritage and History Society and University of Worcester History Students	
4	How Women Kept the Home Fires Burning	58
	The Pershore Women's Institute	
5	Preserving Fruit and Making Jam	72
	Susanne Atkin	
6	Not All Jam and Jerusalem: Pershore Women's Institute	85
	The Pershore Women's Institute	
7	Pershore's Children at War	97
	Emily Linney and University of Worcester History Students	
8	Life Goes on in Pershore	110
	Pershore Heritage and History Society and University of Worcester History Students	
	Further Reading	126
	Index	128

ABOUT THE EDITORS

∽◑◐∾

PROFESSOR MAGGIE ANDREWS is a cultural historian at the University of Worcester. Her research and publications explore women and domesticity in Britain in the twentieth century focusing particularly on the home front in the First and Second World Wars. She leads the theme of 'Gender and the Home Front' for the Voices of War and Peace: The Great War and its Legacy WWI Engagement Centre funded by the Arts & Humanities Research Council (AHRC) and is the historical advisor to the BBC Radio 4 drama *Home Front*.

JENNI WAUGH is a freelance archivist and historian who works with heritage organisations and community groups across the West Midlands to uncover the histories hidden in their localities. Significant projects include BBC People's War, World of Kays and Abberley Lives. She is currently working with Pershore WI, Pershore Heritage and History Society, and the University of Worcester on WW1 in the Vale (HLF-funded) and Volunteers & Voters (AHRC-funded).

ACKNOWLEDGEMENTS

This book has been produced and written by and with many people and groups in and around Pershore, who have researched, discussed, explored and learnt about the history of Pershore in the First World War. They include:

- Pershore Heritage and History Society: Cynthia Johnson (Chair), Roy Albutt, Nancy Fletcher, Heather Greenhalgh, Jean and Tom Haynes, Audrey Humberstone, Margaret Tacy.
- Pershore Women's Institute: Audrey Whitehouse (President), Maureen Speight, Viv Breed, Eileen Rampke, Beth Milsom, Jean Barton.
- Croome Park Volunteer: Susanne Atkin.
- Pershore Civic Society: Judy Dale (Chair).
- Pershore Town Council: Ann Dobbins (Clerk), Tony Rowley (Mayor of Pershore 2014–2016).
- Pershore Library (Worcestershire County Libraries Service): Emma Powell and Helen Faizey.
- Postgraduate and undergraduate history students from the University of Worcester who provided research support and helped out at events, Jess Ball, Darren Tafft, Elspeth King, Emily Linney, Emmanuel Newman, Kenny Peterson, Nikki Primer, Phillip Rose.

The research has been supported by the Heritage Lottery Fund's (HLF) 'First World War: Then & Now' grant programme, the University of Worcester, and the Voices of War and Peace: The Great War and its Legacy WWI Engagement Centre funded by the Arts & Humanities Research Council (AHRC).

The HLF's 'First World War: Then & Now' funding stream provides grants of between £3,000 and £10,000 for community groups to research, conserve and share the often unrecorded local heritage of the First World War (www.hlf.org.uk/looking-funding/our-grant-programmes/first-world-war-then-and-now).

In 2015, HLF awarded grants to both the Pershore Heritage and History Society and the Pershore Women's Institute for a two-year community history project: WW1 in the Vale. For further information about the WW1 in the Vale project and for stories we could not fit into this book, see our blog: ww1inthevale.wordpress. com. The HLF also supports the Worcestershire World War 100 Project (www. ww1worcestershire.co.uk/).

The AHRC-funded 'Voices of War and Peace: the Great War and its Legacy First World War Engagement Centre' is led by the University of Birmingham and works in partnership with the HLF to offer research support and guidance to community groups around the First World War in general and in particular around the following themes: Belief and the Great War, Childhood, Cities at War, Commemoration, Gender and the Home Front (www.voicesofwarandpeace.org).

We are indebted for several of the images in this book to the late Dr Marshall Wilson, who was born in Pershore in 1931. He joined his father as a GP in Pershore and retired in 1991. One of his great interests was research into local history, tracing families and properties back as far as he could. Many Pershore people gave him old photos of forebears or local places and events and these form part of his legacy to Pershore – the Marshall Wilson Collection.

Many of the images, stories and items mentioned in this book can be viewed at the Pershore Heritage Centre, in the Town Hall, Pershore. The Centre is run by volunteers from the Pershore Heritage and History Society and is open from April to October. For full access details see the Society's website: www.pershoreheritage.co.uk/.

This is not a definitive history of Pershore in the First World War, but a starting point, which we hope will enthuse people in the town and in other rural areas to find out more about some of the very varied and often forgotten histories of life on the home front during this conflict.

INTRODUCTION

Pershore is a small market town in South Worcestershire, bordered to the east and south by the River Avon. The elegant Georgian architecture of the main street is evidence of a time when stagecoaches stopped at the many taverns on the road from Worcester to Evesham and London. Just over 100 years ago, in 1911, the town had a population of a little over 4,000 people, swollen on market day when many of those who lived in the surrounding villages and the nearby Vale of Evesham came to Pershore to sell their produce, visit the doctor or shop in the bustling high street.

Four miles to the west lies Croome Park, family seat of George, ninth Earl of Coventry, Lord Lieutenant of Worcestershire, and his wife Blanche, both of whom

Pershore High Street. (Marshall Wilson Collection)

Croome Park today. (Susanne Atkin)

The Earl and Countess of Coventry. (From a supplement to the Worcester Herald, *30 January 1915)*

took an active role in events of both the town and the county, although they were both in their seventies.

At the outbreak of the First World War, Pershore Abbey dominated the skyline of the town, as it still does. The abbey, which dates back to the eleventh century, houses Pershore's memorial to the First World War, a striking bronze statue of Immortality atop a slender column covered with names. Most cities, towns and villages have some sort of memorial – a hall, a park, or most commonly, a stone or bronze statue or tablet, often situated in the market square or at a prominent junction – and almost all bear a list of those who sacrificed their lives fighting in the First World War. However, this conflict was not only fought in the battle-torn lands, skies or seas of Flanders, Serbia, Egypt, Italy or Turkey but also in the factories, kitchens and fields on the home front. When the servicemen went to war other men, women and children were left behind who worried and waited, and worked hard in agriculture and industry, in their homes, in their towns and villages. Without their efforts the conflict would have had a very different outcome.

This book explores what life was like for the residents of Pershore and the surrounding district in wartime. People such as Sydney Falkner, a carter in his thirties, who cultivated 10½ acres of land, and his mother Eliza, who ran the New Inn in Pershore, or Miss Gertrude Annie Chick, a 37-year-old dressmaker living

Pershore Abbey. (Jenni Waugh)

Aerial view of Pershore in the mid-twentieth century. (Pershore Heritage Centre)

in Wisteria Cottage, or Mrs Jane Twivey, the 60-year-old wife of a farm labourer, who lived in New Road. Sidney, Gertrude, Jane and many others had their lives disrupted and utterly altered by the conflict, for, as will be discussed later in the book, they not only tried to keep the 'home fires burning' but they also produced, preserved and prepared the food with which both the nation and the army were fed. Without their efforts, and those of millions like them, Britain could not have won the First World War.

Britain in the early twentieth century was far from self-sufficient in food, having instead a heavy reliance on imports. Nearly 80 per cent of the country's grain, an essential ingredient in bread, the staple food in the working-class diet, was imported from the USA.[1] Two thirds of the sugar, both an important preservative and source of energy, came from the Austro-Hungarian Empire. The first few days of the war saw panic buying, price rises and shortages that became more intense as war progressed. The threat to merchant shipping and food imports caused by the increasing ferocity of submarine warfare in 1917 led to shortages and lengthy queues for food. The following year rationing was introduced in Britain for the very first time. The weekly allowance for each person was 15oz (425 grams) of meat, 5oz (142 grams) of bacon, and 4oz (113 grams) of butter or margarine.[2] Sugar was rationed although bread was not, and there was increasing pressure on

The War Memorial in Pershore Abbey. (Jenni Waugh)

Families picking plums in Pershore. (Marshall Wilson Collection)

the public to eat less bread. These strictures required the whole population to eat less food and the rural population to increase the amount they produced to feed both the armed forces abroad and the civilian population at home. Servicemen fighting overseas had to be supplied with 3,000 calories per man per day. Farmers in Pershore, like others across the country, increased grain production during the conflict, but the smallholders and fruit-growers of the district had another, more significant, role to play in feeding the nation and its fighting forces.

In the early twentieth century, Pershore, Evesham and the villages of the Vale were famous for growing fruit and vegetables. The surrounding hills of Malvern, Bredon and the Cotswolds protected the area from the wind and in Pershore the temperature was usually found to be a little higher than in neighbouring counties. These conditions enabled fruit to ripen up to one month earlier than elsewhere. Pershore was particularly renowned for its local plums, which had been developed in the nineteenth century by grafting new varieties onto fruit trees growing in the ancient Tiddesley Woods to the west of the town. The Pershore Purple was a small, tart plum, ideal for bottling, canning and pickling. The large yellow Pershore egg plum was particularly useful for jam making and provided the key ingredient for the apple and plum jam provided to the troops at the Front, which became notorious during the conflict.

Over 4,000 acres of land in Worcestershire were dedicated to plum growing in the pre-war era and Pershore was particularly well appointed to play a major role in fruit production and preservation during the conflict. Two jam and pulping factories were in operation in the town by 1914. Pershore station was on the main line between

Hereford and London Paddington, and it was therefore easy for growers to transport fruit, vegetables and jam quickly to other major conurbations such as Birmingham and Bristol. Indeed, in 1906 one of the leading local growers had observed, 'We have an almost perfect train service to every part of the kingdom'.[3]

As the fresh produce left Pershore by rail, so a wide range of newcomers arrived at the station: Belgian refugees, prisoners of war, Boy Scouts, university students, schoolboys. All manner of volunteers came to assist in the cultivation and harvest of fruit and vegetables needed to win the war.

The importance of Pershore plums was trumpeted around the world, as can be seen from this article, which was published in a newspaper in Nelson, New Zealand:

GIRLS IN THE PLUM TREES

Plum and Apple jam has become a standard joke in the army, and considering that hundreds of tons of it are consumed every day by our troops it is rather interesting to hear where the vast quantity of fruit comes from.

I (a correspondent in a London Journal) used to wonder until I went plum picking in Worcestershire and realised that three quarters of this beautiful county is given up to the cultivation of the fruit. Devonshire, Somersetshire and Herefordshire may claim the apples but Worcestershire has no rival for plums.

Harvesting Pershore plums. (Marshall Wilson Collection)

Like many similar jobs now successfully accomplished by women, in pre-war days it was considered 'men's work' but if the women did not do it now 'Tommy' would be without his jam ration. The slight element of danger makes it all the more fascinating.

There are numberless varieties of plums which come into season quickly one after the other, but those which make the best jam are the 'Pershore' or 'Yellow Egg' kind. Some of the fruit trees grow tall and straight with long, thin, wavering branches which are not easy to reach; some are thick and bushy; some grow like date palms and are very difficult and rather dangerous to pick; others are so dense that the branches scratch our faces and uproot our hair.

The first thing we had to learn was how to 'set' our ladders properly. It is courting disaster to trust in the trunk of plum trees, and we need to choose the thickest and leafiest bough and plant our ladders nearly upright against it, so the combined weight of ourselves and the ladder is rested principally on the ground, and not the bough itself.

As both hands were required for picking the fruit we fastened very large baskets round our waists by leather straps when we went up the trees. The baskets were then emptied into sacks which had to contain 60lbs of the fruit, and these we dragged along the lines between the trees to be 'weighed up.' There must often have been 'fruit pulp' ready at the bottom of the sacks after we had pulled them over the rough and stony ground.

The Nelson Evening Mail, 16 November 1918

This account from 1918 reflects the experience of many fruit-pickers throughout the war, both local residents and volunteers from out of town. To find out how the Pershore fruit trade became so renowned, this book will begin by looking at how this small market town was affected by the outbreak of war and how farmers struggled to meet the challenge of increasing food production when many young men had gone to fight a war. The changes the conflict brought to ordinary people's lives will then be discussed, the need to preserve the fruit and, finally, how the war affected the lives of women and children.

This book is about one small community in Worcestershire,[4] and yet it is about so very much more than that. It is about the need to imagine what it was like to live through the First World War on the home front. For across the country there were thousands of residents in rural towns and villages producing food and knitting socks, just as they did in Pershore and the Vale of Evesham. They all played a unique, although often forgotten, part in winning the war.

NOTES

1 P.E. Dewey, *British Agriculture in the First World War* (Oxford: Routledge 1989, reprinted 2014)

2 L.M. Barnett, *British Food Policy During the First World War* (Oxford: Routledge 1985, reprinted 2014)

3 R.C. Gaut, *A History of Worcestershire Agriculture and Rural Evolution* (Worcester: Littlebury Press, 1939)

4 M. Andrews, A. Gregson and J. Peters, *Voices of the First World War: Worcestershire's War* (Stroud: Amberley Press, 2014)

1

WAR COMES to PERSHORE

Emily Linney and University of Worcester
History Students

The First World War began on 4 August 1914 and according to the *Evesham Journal*, Europe was faced with the 'most tremendous war in the history of the world', which meant that 'she has been forced to take up arms'. The consequences of the conflict were felt immediately in the town: Pershore Horticultural Show was abandoned and, at the Abbey Church, special prayers were offered for peace at the Sunday service. A round-up of local news reported:

POSITION IN PERSHORE

Preparations are making rapid strides to provide for families whose breadwinners are serving in the war. It is a noticeable fact that considering the size of the town, an unusually large number of men have gone to serve their King and country. They include members of the outdoor staff of the Post Office who were on reserve, a police officer, several men from the Atlas Works and a large number of market gardeners. Many are holding themselves to be called upon at any moment, and others from local banks have volunteered for various branches … Many ladies are busily preparing themselves to go as nurses under the Red Cross Association being members of the local First Aid Detachments. Other ladies are assisting in making shirts and other garments for the soldiers.

Worcester Herald, 15 August 1914

Recruitment

Until conscription was introduced in 1916, the men in the armed forces who were sent to fight had all volunteered to join.[1] During August and September 1914, a number of recruitment drives took place in earnest in Pershore, intended to increase their number. Lord Coventry, who had been appointed Lord Lieutenant of the county in 1891 and Honorary Colonel of the Worcestershire Regiment in 1900, took an interest in all matters military. On the day war was declared, he took part in an 'interesting ceremony at Croome Park':

NEW COLOURS FOR WORCESTER REGIMENT

Lord Coventry, the honorary colonel, presented new colours on Tuesday to the 5th Battalion of the Worcestershire Regiment, who have for some time been in camp on his lordship's estate, Croome Park. The ceremony was shorn of much of its effectiveness by the weather, heavy downpours occurring during the parade and on the return march to camp …

The new colours presented on Tuesday were dedicated by the Rev. W. W. Veness. and were handed to the officers by Lord Coventry, who was accompanied by the Countess of Coventry, Viscount Deerhurst and the house party.

He addressed the battalion, stating […] the record of the regiment's service was one of which the county might well be proud … They all hoped sincerely that recruiting might be helped.

Gloucestershire Echo, 5 August 1914

In the days following this ceremony, soldiers already enlisted drilled in the town, and were inspected by Lord Coventry, in the hope that this would 'stimulate' many young fellows to 'offer themselves for their country'. It was envisaged that once the harvests had been gathered more young men would be free to join up. Veterans of the Boer War, such as Mr Hugh Mumford, volunteered again for service. A large recruitment meeting was held at the Music Hall, source of much of the popular entertainment in the town, where, only months earlier, German pianist Isabel Hirschfeld had been welcomed to play a benefit concert for the Boy Scouts.

RECRUITMENT MEETING AT PERSHORE

A meeting was held at the Music Hall on Tuesday evening being called by the joint Parish Councils of Holy Cross and St Andrew's for the purpose of aiding recruitment in the district. The room was packed … The platform was perfectly decorated with flags. Lord Deerhurst [Lord Coventry's eldest son and a serving soldier] was greeted with applause, said they were meeting to get recruits for Lord Kitchener's Army. For years we had been proud to think we had a voluntary system (hear, hear). We said if England wanted men there were millions who would lay down their lives for her. It was up to people to demonstrate that this was a fact. The country was in need of young men …

Poster for the Isabel Hirschfield concert at the Music Hall. (Jenni Waugh)

Admiral Cuming in a rousing speech said the war was the greatest ever known. We have been forced into it to protect a weaker nation like Belgium, and England was calling every man must do his duty.

Mr T.W. Parker said that as a man who took part in the public life of the district he would like to say a few words. He did not think they needed words, for he had good faith in the young men of Pershore and district. He appealed to the young men to come forward and join.

Col A.H. Hudson said he was sure Pershore men would respond to the appeal for recruits. There had been more than 90 recruits from Pershore district during the last few days ... The Rev. F.R. Lawson, Rector of Fladbury, said he would ask the forgiveness of the speakers on the platform when he said they should honour not so much the men who made great speeches as the lad who went and fought for his country and mother who let him go. (Applause). At the close of the meeting, a large number gave in their names to enlist in the various branches of the Army.

The Music Hall as it is today. (Roy Albutt)

EXCELLENT RESPONSE AT PERSHORE

A large number of able-bodied men have offered themselves for service. The Recruiting Officer, Sgt J.J. Cook, has been inundated ... Batches of about 30 per day have been dispatched to Norton Barracks for transfer to various depots. The recruits have, with few exceptions, come up to the standard demanded, and have been conveyed to the railway station in motor cars kindly lent by gentlemen in the district.

Worcester Herald, 12 September 1914

By this point a number of young men had already joined up, nevertheless, in late November about 250 soldiers of Captain Warren Hudson's company visited Pershore on a route march to stimulate further recruitment. Just as these young men of Pershore set off to war, so Belgian refugees, victims of the conflict, began to arrive in the district.

Belgian refugees

Between the months of September and December 1914, 250,000 Belgian refugees entered Britain, fleeing the German invasion of their homeland. At the time, this was the largest flood of people that had arrived into Britain.[2] Initially arriving in

Laughern House in Pershore as it looks today. (Heather Greenhalgh)

Folkestone, Kent, the refugees soon moved to accommodation in towns and villages across the country. In Worcestershire they were billeted in Pershore, Evesham and many of the surrounding villages, such as Eckington, Fladbury, Elmley Castle, Great Comberton and Defford.

The residents of Pershore and Evesham responded to the news that refugees would be brought to their area in a number of ways. Donations of money, furniture, and even houses were made to accommodate refugee families. The Revd Lawson of Fladbury sat up a Coordinating Committee at Pershore to provide hospitality in the area, on which Archdeacon Peile sat as Chairman. On 21 October 1914, during a well-attended public meeting to discuss the procedures for accepting Belgian refugees, the committee decided that thirty could be accommodated. Mr J.R. Lacy offered Laughern House for twenty refugees and undertook to be responsible for their maintenance.

REFUGEES AT PERSHORE

Great interest was shown by the townspeople in the arrival of the first batch of Belgian refugees. They came to Laughern House, in Bridge Street, the residence recently purchased by Mr J.R. Lacy, a Birmingham solicitor, who not only has granted free use of the spacious premises, but is also generously providing for their maintenance. The furniture has mostly been lent by townspeople, and the house is adequately and comfortably furnished for the accommodation of the visitors. Mrs Arthur Baker, with the assistance of Miss A. Matthews, has kindly consented to supervising the catering arrangements.

Flags were put up at some of the houses in the street, and a crowd awaited their arrival and greeted them with cheers. The refugees were conveyed from Defford station at five o'clock in the evening in Mr Burnham's motor cars. Among those who went to meet them were the Rev. Father Norman Holly, of Pershore (who also has arranged to put up at his own house a Belgian journalist and his son and a Flemish priest).

Evesham Journal, 31 October 1914

The number of refugees under the charge of the committee varied, but in the first six months fifty-eight were maintained, including twenty in Pershore, fifteen in Eckington and ten in Fladbury. Initially, as the newspaper report suggests, these refugees were accorded a warm welcome in Pershore. A range of fund-raising activities were organised for the Belgian Relief Fund, including a social entertainment at Throckmorton. The Coordinating Committee stressed their gratitude to the many kind helpers, especially the women, who were looking after the refugees, whilst acknowledging the issues these volunteers were facing as many of the refugees spoke neither French nor English.

REFUGEES IN PERSHORE

Two Belgian victims of German 'Kulture' who after grave mental and physical suffering are finding hospitality and quiet rest at the home of Father Norman Holly, Roman Catholic Priest at Pershore, are a Flemish priest and his housekeeper.

The Rev. Vital Nichoul, a man of refined and gentle aspect, was rector of Hever, a village three miles from the ill-fated town of Malines. On 22 August, he having business to transact and his housekeeper having shopping to do they went together to Malines expecting to return in the afternoon. But news of the near approach of the Germans arrived, and the town was seething with excitement. With thousands of others they were compelled by the military authorities to flee. The rev[erend] gentleman has lost well nigh everything.

Evening Journal, 7 November 1914

Within two weeks, the Revd Vital Nichoul was recalled from this comfortable billet to Belgium by his bishop. Other refugees received a chillier welcome, as it was felt they could not contribute to the needs of agriculture in the locality:

PERSHORE AND THE BELGIANS

Not being of the class that was particularly asked for, neither proving themselves amiable to the necessary rules and regulations set up by the three Flemish sisters installed in Laughern House, the residence generously lent by Mr J.R. Lacy, the fifteen Belgian refugees who only arrived about ten days ago have been transferred to a colony of their own countrymen at Warwick. Application has again been made to the Birmingham Committee for a contingent consisting of agricultural labourers, and these it is thought will arrive in a few days.

Evesham Journal, 7 November 1914

A fortnight later the *Evesham Journal* reported that a family of nine had come to live in Laughern House: 'a prominent business man of Antwerp, his wife and six children and a maid, a ruined family, everything gone except the few little things they were able to collect before hastily fleeing from the bombarded city.' Some support for the refugees came from further afield. In November 1914, a significant donation of supplies came from Mrs Barrow Cadbury of Edgbaston, Birmingham, who gifted fifty bedsteads, fifty beds, fifty blankets, and fifty pillows to refugees located in Pershore, estimated to have cost £40 (roughly equivalent to £1,700 today). She was a trustee of the Cadbury Institute in Birmingham, which had also been helping refugees.

There were attempts to provide a degree of normality for the Belgian refugees. The *Evesham Journal* reported on the decision to allocate work to refugees: men were offered a minimum weekly wage of 15s and women, 9s. According to *The Pershore Almanac*, of the forty-five refugees under the Pershore Committee, all of the men were employed by 4 November 1914, and their work on the land was expected to increase the labour needed for future harvests. However, in October 1914, when, with 'good intentions', two Belgians were treated to beer from a local public house, one reportedly became troublesome; the magistrates were told that the men were unused to drinking alcohol and were overcome by the quantities that they drank. While this case suggests that local people attempted to welcome refugees, the local paper subsequently published a warning against 'the public treating of refugees with strong drink' and the sixty refugees attending the Christmas party at the Masonic Hall in December 1914 were treated only to tea and a Christmas tree.

In Spring 1915, the Chairman of the Belgian Refugee Committee reported that the total sum of money collected to provide aid had reached £891 2s 8d over six months (a staggering sum, worth approximately £38,500 today). £676 15s 3d was accumulated by the many local villagers who agreed to contribute weekly subscriptions to support the forty-five refugees under the care of the committee. School logbooks recorded that local school children were also helping 'needy Belgian refugees' in more direct ways: following a talk on the plight of the Belgians, pupils at St Mary's Church of England School in Hanley Castle knitted blankets and held a school fête, which raised £1 15s 10d for the Belgian Relief Fund (approximately £78 today). There were, however, some indications that the initial hospitality and enthusiasm felt towards refugees began to wane over time. This was alluded to in the Chairman of the Pershore Relief Committee's report on 19 May 1915 when he appealed for subscribers' 'continued and renewed support'. After six months, the committee had begun to query how much longer the Belgians would need their help and, indeed, a party left Alveston House in Pershore at the end of March 1915 whilst another two families had already gone back to London.

The growing awareness of the realities of war

Within a few months of the outbreak of war, it was not just the arrival of the Belgian refugees who made the scale and consequences of the conflict clear to the people of Pershore. Letters began to arrive from servicemen to their families, many of which were then published in the local newspapers, the *Evesham Journal* particularly. Postman Percy Smith wrote home to his mother after being injured at Zeebouges (*sic*), Belgium. Recovering from a head wound in a hospital in Aberdeen, Scotland, he stated that he 'really thought his time had come' and had 'waited three hours for death'. He notes that 'six of my pals have gone' and his letter, printed in the *Evesham Journal* on 19 November 1914, is full of melancholy horror: 'the scenes are indescribable,' 'many say it isn't war; it's murder with the guns' and he writes that he has killed a few of the Uhlans (Prussian troops). Before this letter was even published Pershore had received news of the first local casualty of war:

CASUALTIES TO LOCAL OFFICERS

The family of Lieut. Aubrey W. Hudson, who was reported missing on Sept. 28, have now received an official intimation that he is dead. He was the youngest son of Col. A.H. Hudson, of Wick, Pershore, and 31 years of age. He served for several years with the Cape Mounted Rifles in South Africa under Col. Lukin. Transferred in 1909 to the 5th Worcesters, he was appointed to the 2nd Battalion for active service.

At a meeting of the Pershore Board of Guardians on Tuesday the members passed a vote of condolence with Col. Hudson and his family. Two other sons of Col. Hudson (who is a director of the Cheltenham Original Brewery Co.), are serving with the Army.

Gloucestershire Echo, 7 October 1914

Lieutenant Hudson, whose father had taken such an active role in the recruitment drive in Pershore, was killed at Aisne on 20 September 1914 and his memorial now stands in Wick parish church. His family lost two other young men during the war: Aubrey's brother, Captain Arthur Cyril Hudson of the 7th Royal Fusiliers, died of his wounds at Boulogne in October 1916, and his cousin, Lieutenant Alban

Memorial for Lieutenant Hudson in Wick church. (Jenni Waugh)

Hudson, was killed at the Battle of Messines in June 1917. However, Aubrey's other brother, Major William Warren Hudson of 11th Worcesters, returned home at the end of the war.

Within days, notice of Sergeant Charles Stevenson's death on 31 October was delivered to his mother Martha, postmistress at Wick. An even more visible reminder of the costs of war was provided by the men sent home, either temporarily to recover from injuries sustained or because they were permanently disabled. There were two medical establishments in Pershore at this time: the Cottage Hospital on Defford Road, and the Sanatorium (alias Fever or Isolation Hospital) on Three Springs Road. Neither appear to have accepted military casualties; perhaps because the medical officer from the Cottage Hospital had himself left to join the forces.

SERGT. C. STEVENSON (WICK, PERSHORE), 2nd BATT. ESSEX REGT., KILLED IN ACTION OCTOBER 31.
(Photo Dowty, Pershore.)

Sergeant C. Stevenson of the 2nd Battalion, Essex Regiment, who was killed in action.

*Avonbank Convalescent Home.
(Marshall Wilson Collection)*

For Pershore residents, life on the home front was not free from death and illness. Infections such as scarlet fever, diphtheria and tuberculosis caused problems for the townspeople as did a range of agricultural accidents and other disasters. The Cottage Hospital had only thirteen beds and the Sanatorium less, so despite gifts of potatoes, peas, broad beans, books and newspapers from local residents, the staff may have felt they were already stretched. Nevertheless, Avonbank, home of the Marriott family and latter the site of the Horticultural College, was turned into a convalescent home for soldiers recovering from illness or injuries caused by their participation in war. Convalescing soldiers would have become a familiar sight around the town in their distinctive bright blue uniform with a red collar to ensure no one mistook them for civilians unwilling to fight.

The local newspapers were not censored and thus brought the most vivid descriptions of the realities of war to those at home. Perhaps one of the most traumatic stories appeared in the local newspaper in March 1915:

EVESHAM MAN SHOT AS A DESERTER

As there are many rumours in the town with regard to the death of an Evesham soldier named Albert Pitts … Mrs Pitts of 22, Kings-Road Bengeworth, asks us to publish the facts of the case as she knows them. In the last week of November Mrs Pitts received a letter from her husband, in which he stated 'I have been lost for two weeks, but I have got on the right track for the regiment … I can only say I am writing this from Calais only twenty-one miles from old England …'.

On December 1st he wrote 'It leaves me quite well at present, except my ears. I am gone quite deaf now, but I think it will go off. I have been struggling along. I have not had a chance to find my regiment, for you cannot understand the French. They direct you wrong, but I shall find them just now.'

On 21 January he wrote a letter which he addressed from his company of the Warwickshire Regiment. In this letter he said he did not receive the Christmas parcel his wife sent. This letter was endorsed as follows: 'Pte Pitts was absent during Christmas without leave and naturally his present did not reach him – Censor'.

Mrs Pitts heard nothing further until Wednesday morning this week when she received the following letter: – 'Infantry Record Office … March 2nd 1915 – Madam No 6747 Pte Alfred Pitts 2nd Battalion Royal Warwickshire Regiment was sentenced after trial by court martial to be shot for "when on active service" deserting His Majesty's Service, and the sentence was duly executed on February 8th 1915 at 7.30am. R.F. Formby Lieut.-Col …'

Yesterday morning Mrs Pitts received the following letter from her husband:

'My dearest wife and kiddies – Just a few lines in answer to your loving letter I received quite safe. Well, I expect this will be the last letter from me, my dear as I have got to be shot for being absent: but I could not help it. I tried to find my regiment. I did my very best, but it can't be helped. My dear I wish I could have seen you all. You must try to do your best for the kiddies. I should not upset myself. My dear, I did my duty before I was absent. It has all been trouble with us. I was very unlucky. I am so sorry to have to write a letter like this, my dear: I am quite done up. I did not think I should have come to an end like this, dear. I would rather be shot by a German. Well I must close now darling, for the last time. Try to forget me, for your broken-hearted husband, Bert. Do your best for my dear kiddies. God Bless them. May He be always with you and them'. Here follows a number of crosses that represent kisses.

Mrs Pitts has three young children, the eldest seven years of age. Pitts has served twelve years with the Warwicks and was a reservist at the outbreak of hostilities, when he signed on for another four years.

Evesham Journal, 6 March 1915

As Albert Pitts was shot as a deserter, his wife would not have received a pension and her struggle to bring up three children in the years that followed would have been a hard one.

NOTES

1   For a more detailed exploration of recruitment and volunteering in the First World War see A. Gregory, *The Last Great War: British Society and the First World War* (Cambridge: Cambridge University Press, 2008) or N. Mansfield, *English Farmworkers and Local Patriotism, 1900–1930* (Basingstoke: Ashgate, 2001).

2   Further discussion of Belgian refugees can be found in T. Kushner, *Remembering Refugees: Then and Now* (Manchester: MUP, 2006).

2

GROWING FOOD IN THE MARKET GARDENS AND FARMS OF PERSHORE

Pershore Heritage and History Society and
University of Worcester History Students

⟨⟨⟩⟩

At the outbreak of the First World War, organisers of food production for the war effort were able to call upon the various forms of agriculture and horticulture already established in Britain[1]. In Worcestershire, known as the 'home of the smallholder', there were nearly 3,000 units of between 1 and 5 acres; 75 per cent of the county's agriculture was tied up in small farms under 50 acres. This system had developed because the 1908 Small Holdings and Allotments Act had allowed local authorities to buy up farms and divide them into smallholdings for rent, something Worcestershire County Council did with determination, acquiring over 50,000 acres in this way.[2]

Fruit and vegetable growing in cottage gardens and on local allotments complemented food production in smallholdings. When the Besford Court Estate in Defford was sold in October 1914, it was broken into over 100 lots intended to appeal to prospective market gardeners and smallholders. A large variety of fruit was grown in the area, often alongside arable farming. For example, in 1916, the 200 acres owned by Mr Deakin, the jam manufacturer who lived at Pershore Hall, included 21 acres of arable whilst the rest was fruit plantation. Likewise, fruit-growing was not always the owner's sole occupation. Adverts for the sale or lease of smallholdings in 1914 suggested the land could provide either a part-time or full-time income and military tribunals from 1916 similarly indicate that men often worked smallholdings alongside other paid work: one applicant described himself as 'a printer and a market gardener', Thomas Bourne was a butcher, farmer and fruit grower in Drake's Broughton, and Leonard Edgar Westcott was a smallholder and sub-postmaster at Pinvin. These smaller market gardens relied upon family labour and were finely balanced small subsistence agricultural units, with plum, apple and other fruit trees, often under-planted with vegetables, enabling quite modest-sized market gardens to be intensively farmed.

The efficient sale of the produce of numerous small growers needed a fair degree of organisation. Pickers would fill woven 'pot hampers' with fruit and vegetables, which would be taken to market and sold to wholesalers. Pot sizes varied from district to district and according to the produce being collected. In Pershore the convention was 40lb pots of beans, peas and sprouts, 72lbs of plums or pears and 64lbs of apples.

The pots were stamped with the initials PPPP which stood for 'Pershore Produce Properly Packed', understood locally as 'Pershore People Poorly Paid'.

Advert for Spiers baskets from the Pershore Fruit Growers Directory of 1915. (Pershore Heritage Centre)

J. M. Spiers,

CABINET MAKER, UPHOLSTERER AND BASKET MANUFACTURER,

Bridge St., Pershore.

ALL KINDS OF FURNITURE MADE TO ORDER.

Carpets supplied and planned to room.
Bedsteads and Bedding.   Mattresses cleaned and re-made.
Window Draperies, Cornices, Venetian, Sun
and all kinds of Blinds supplied and fitted.

FURNITURE REPAIRED AND REPOLISHED

EQUAL TO NEW.

Pershore pot hamper. (Pershore Heritage Centre)

Printing
—FOR—
Fruit Growers.

Duplicate Consignment Books, Postcard and Memo Books, Price Lists, Envelopes, Etc., at Lowest Competitive Prices.

LABELS.

Letter Paper and Post Cards.
Fruit Packing Paper.
Greaseproof. Tissues, Newspapers, etc.
Blue Packing Paper.
Hamper Covers for Pots, Half-Pots, Sieves, and Chips.
Corrugated Paper.   Collapsible Cardboard Boxes.
Hemp, White and Coloured Twines, and General Fruit Growers' Sundries.

FEARNSIDE & MARTIN,
Printers & Stationers,
AVON HOUSE, PERSHORE.

Advert for Labels in the Pershore Fruit Growers Directory of 1915. (Pershore Heritage Centre)

Advert for fruit boxes, crates and trays in the Pershore Fruit Growers Directory of 1915. (Pershore Heritage Centre)

P. Burns Conly & Son,
General Carpenters.
G.W.R. Station, PERSHORE.

FRUIT BOXES, CRATES AND TRAYS
ALL SIZES.

Ladders, Hovels, Poultry Houses, Wheelbarrows, Loganberry Fences, Frames, Greenhouses, etc., etc.

FREE ESTIMATES ON APPLICATION.

Broad Street market. (Marshall Wilson Collection)

Local family company J.M. Spiers were famous for their willow baskets. During the war, wounded soldiers helped to make the pots and in July 1916, 41-year-old Edward Hitchcox, a married basket maker who lived in York Cottage, Pershore, was conditionally exempted from military service because of the importance of his work to the war effort. Other local industries supporting fruit production in the town included producers of labels and crates.

The Pershore Co-operative Market

The fame, popularity and significance of Pershore's plums owed a great deal to the town's unique Co-operative Market. The Pershore Fruit Growers' & Market Gardeners' Association was formed in 1907 to enable 400 small fruit growers in the district to compete with the larger producers in the area. After some initial teething problems,

> The first fruit and vegetable market worked in England by the co-operative principle was opened recently at Pershore … the venture was registered under the Industrial and Provident Societies Act. It is pleasing to be able to record that the market opened in a most satisfactory way. There was plenty of the best produce the district can produce and many buyers, some having come from long distances. At present the sales are held in Broad Street, but it is likely that before long they will take place in a more desirable venue. The market day is Thursday.
>
> *Gloucestershire Echo*, 3 July 1909

Postcard showing the Co-operative Market building. (Susanne Atkin)

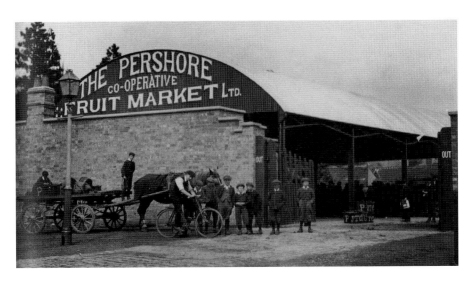

Pershore Co-Operative Market. (Cynthia Johnson)

By the following year,

> A new building erected for the Pershore Co-operative Fruit Market was opened on Thursday. The market is the first co-operative fruit market in the country, and it met with sufficient success in the first year's trading to encourage hopes of developments in the future.
>
> … a convenient site was obtained on the Defford road close to Broad-street. There a market similar to the markets at Evesham has been erected at a cost between £500 and £600. The site occupies 1,700 square yards.
>
> *Cheltenham Chronicle*, 30 April 1910

There was praise in the *Gloucester Evening Echo* on 1 May 1914 for those 'few men with the business instinct' who ran the market 'eager to adopt the latest changes which scientific research and business expediency dictate'. Those men included Geoffrey Fielder Hooper: inaugural President of the Co-Operative until 1918, Chairman of the Fruit Growers' & Market Gardeners' Association and on the Management Committee of the County Evening Instruction of Gardeners. Brought up in London and educated at Marlborough, Hooper moved to Pershore in the 1890s to study fruit farming under Alderman Henry Masters of Benge Hill, Evesham. When the war broke out he and his wife and daughter lived at The Croft, on Station Road, surrounded by 28 acres of market garden.

When he died in 1932, Hooper was described in the *Cheltenham Chronicle* on 28 May as 'one of the largest and best employers of labour in the district', a 'pioneer

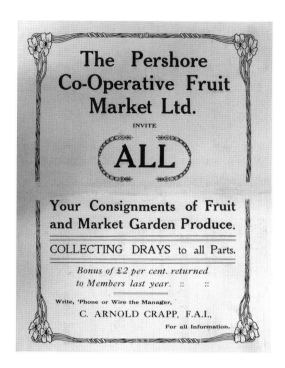

The Pershore Co-Operative Fruit Market Ltd.

INVITE

ALL

Your Consignments of Fruit and Market Garden Produce.

COLLECTING DRAYS to all Parts.

Bonus of £2 per cent. returned to Members last year. :: ::

Write, 'Phone or Wire the Manager,

C. ARNOLD CRAPP, F.A.I.,

For all Information.

of scientific fruit growing' whose market garden was a model 'of good husbandry and up-to-date methods of cultivation'. He was a pillar of the community, a churchwarden and committee man; a self-publicist seldom reluctant to put pen to paper on behalf of Pershore fruit growers. With his large house, domestic servants and agricultural employees, Hooper could be seen as representative of the wealthier market gardeners in the district and under his guidance the Co-operative Market's reputation grew:

> Small growers in the district have felt the benefit. Many of them prefer to receive what they see their produce sold for (less 7½ per cent, commission) rather than to take the risks of sending to the big markets.
>
> *Cheltenham Chronicle,* 29 April 1910

That the Market attracted national attention is evident from this extract from a longer article about the publication of the Agricultural Organisation Society Ltd's annual report into the Co-operative Sale of Produce:

> The total number of packages sold before the end of the year was 40,858, and the aggregate price realised was £4,721 [£203,290 today]. The commission earned by the society amounting to £366. In its report for 1909 the committee says

The gravestone of Edith and Geoffrey Hooper in Pershore cemetery. (Roy Albutt)

prices have, generally speaking, been better than those obtained by growers at other local and distant markets …

The co-operative principal had spread throughout the district:

A large business in the collective sale by commission of market garden produce was done by the Littleton & Badsey Growers Ltd, a society composed almost entirely of smallholders. The total sales amounted to £4,648 [just over £200,000 today], on which a profit of £93 was made. The profit would have been larger but for the loss of a large number of baskets, a fact which emphasises the importance of keeping a strict account on all baskets, inwards and outwards, which can be readily accomplished by a careful system of book-keeping.

Sussex Agricultural Express, 30 September 1910

A report in the *Cheltenham Chronicle* in May 1913 claimed the Co-operative Market controlled one-third of the produce grown in the Pershore area, including the villages. The district's methods of growing and organisation were studied and strongly promoted as a beacon of good practice. Pershore was described as 'the most advanced agricultural community in the British Isles'[3] and by May 1914, annual turnover had increased to almost £25,000. Nevertheless, in July 1914 Arthur Beynon, manager of the Pomona Works, was appointed permanent director of a second market, the Central Fruit Market, based at his works in Pershore High Street. Charles Twigg was appointed as agent, as well as three local market gardeners. Jim Dowler, a local resident, remembered that,

There was quite a class distinction between the two markets and the people who went there. In the Central Market there was socialism and in the Co-operative Market there was capitalism.

In the summer of 1914, even as tensions were mounting in Europe, a group of fifty farmers, touring the UK from South Africa and Rhodesia, travelled to Evesham Vale in motor cars decorated with feathers and the flag of the old Boer Republic. They were greeted in a friendly way in many villages and then:

> … motored to Pershore, where they were much interested in the Co-operative Fruit and Vegetable Market. They thought the Co-operative principle might be developed with advantage in South Africa where at present butter factories and cooperation for the sale of mealies are the only enterprises of the kind. They then went over Mr Geoffrey Hooper's fruit farm, and also examined with interest the fifty acres of hops at Wick, some suggesting the feasibility of growing hops in South Africa.
>
> *Birmingham Daily Mail*, 30 June 1914

The two co-operative societies proved invaluable during the war years, enabling smallholders, cottage gardeners, fruit-growers and market gardeners of any scale to sell their produce, although they were aware of the increasing challenges of distribution.

FRUIT AND CROP TRANSPORT DIFFICULTIES

> The Pershore Co-operative Fruit Market is endeavoring to cope with the influx of fruit and vegetables by sending out an appeal to growers, buyers and the railway companies, asking that every effort be made to relieve the strain by getting produce on and off the market as quickly as possible. At a time like the present, when labour is scarce and railway facilities have been curtailed the appeal is needed.
>
> *Worcester Herald*, 1 August 1915

In December 1916, the Pershore Fruit Growers' Association met with Major Belcher of the War Office Canteen Committee. The major asked Pershore farmers and growers to help with supplies, 'which they were eager to provide in order to avoid the government commandeering fruit to meet the needs of the army'. Geoffrey Hooper urged fruit growers to be continually on the lookout for new outlets. In 1915 he wrote in the *Pershore Fruit Growers' Yearbook*: 'Just now there is a wide field in the immense military camps and depots and in the various concentration and prisoners' camps.' Many growers were happy to give preferential treatment to the Army and Navy, but the shortages of labour and resources were challenging.

The fruit market was considered so important that some employees' work was seen as essential to the war effort, and they successfully appealed against conscription:

Charles Clumens, who carried on his late father's coal merchant business in Pershore High Street whilst also working as the clerk to the Pershore Co-operative Fruit Market, and Charles Arnold Crapp, auctioneer and general manager of the Pershore Co-operative Fruit Market, were exempted as was Sidney J. Sharp, a miller of 34 years old who with his brother Harry ran the Wyre Mills, Pershore.

The Pershore Co-operative Fruit Market appealed for Frank Arthur Goodhall, general clerk and assistant auctioneer at the market. His work was with empties (containers for carrying fruit) which was work that was important and complicated. This work proved too challenging for women, who were inexperienced.

Worcester Herald, 23 June 1917

Farmers' problems

The outbreak of war brought a number of challenges for those growing the produce sold in Pershore's markets. Initially, local newspapers reported little impact on railway services and market gardeners distributed their produce 'without trouble'. Nevertheless, anxiety about both transport and the high price of sugar led to a drop in the price of fruit whilst growers expressed concern about how they might cope without the usual imports of seeds, peas and bulbs from Holland, France and Germany. The *Worcester Daily Times* reported concerns over whether sufficient labour would be available to harvest all the fruit in the Vale of Evesham in August 1914. In the following months many men volunteered. There was a strong regimental tradition in the county and a number of men who ran the market gardens had experience of the cadet force or university. By December 1914, the vicar of Fladbury would lament: 'practically all the able-bodied young men of the village had joined the colours.'

Throughout the war, recruitment of adequate labour was the over-arching problem for food producers in the region, exaggerated in Pershore and the Vale because smallholdings and market gardens were so intensively worked. According to the *Yorkshire Evening Post* on 23 November 1916, the land 'is highly cultivated, and the proportion of labour is in the ratio of one man to five acres whereas on other agricultural land the ratio is usually one farm hand to fifty acres'. Some men in the area were reticent about volunteering to fight because they were aware of the strain it would place upon their businesses. Those who ran smallholdings or market gardens, full-time or as a sideline, had a great deal invested in them, which perhaps explains why, on 15 March 1915, the *Cheltenham Echo* reported that not one man volunteered in the village of Bretforton, near Evesham, despite appeals from the recruiting officer, and the reading aloud of a list of twenty-five eligible men was accompanied by accusations of cowardice. Bretforton was the heart of the Vale's asparagus-growing region and all men and women were needed on the smallholdings for the harvest in May. Without the proceeds of the asparagus sales, the long-term viability of family businesses would be threatened. Despite propaganda posters, no women in this village would have 'said go' to their husbands or sons at this time of the year.

The strains were so great that one member of the County Agricultural Advisory Committee expressed the view that he would prefer someone to take his farm and let him fight. Some farmers found the pressure unbearable:

PERSHORE FARMER'S SUICIDE
WORRIED BY ARMY HAY CONTRACT

At the inquest as to the death of Francis Longland (42), of Hurst Farm, Pershore, who shot himself in a barn on Thursday, it was stated that he had been worried about fulfilling his hay contract with the War Office. Major Robinson who is the authorised purchaser of hay for the War Office, attended, and said no pressure had been brought to bear upon the deceased man, and that, after hearing of his inability to complete his contract, he (Major Robinson) released him from the contract. Deceased had said he could not get cutters to get on with their work because he had a lot of drunken workers.

Mrs Edith Longland, the widow, said she went to find her husband, as he did not come in for breakfast, and saw him sitting on the hay in a barn with the gun pointed towards him. She screamed and the gun went off. Deceased had been distressed and worried over the war and also by the fact their son had enlisted. He has had influenza and accidents in the hunting field, which had hurt his head.

Mr H.G. Shepherd, farmer, a friend of Longland, said there was a halter on a beam in the cider house, and evidence that the deceased man had tried to hang himself. On one piece of cigarette-paper on the floor he had written: 'Oh my poor heart, Goodbye all. Cannot see my boy go. All is ruined through this cursed hay.'

The verdict was 'Suicide while temporarily insane'.

Birmingham Daily Post, 19 July 1915

The *Birmingham Post* reported on 30 December 1915 that: 'the labour difficulty is the problem of the day both on garden and farm. During the past year much work had to be left undone which ought to have been done and with considerably fewer hands available growers wonder how they will manage when the busy time comes.' The introduction of conscription in 1916, initially for single men and then married men, placed added pressure on the growers and many found that they were struggling. Farmers like Mr Dee applied to the local tribunal to exempt their men from having to undertake military service. He explained:

Wyles' tractor was designed to go between fruit trees. (Pershore Heritage Centre)

His staff on the 31st July, the month before the war were 12 men, two of whom were elderly and three boys. Now he had only eight men, only three of whom are able bodied …

When asked about the two sons he had at home he responded:

> … that he had three sons on military service. He next appealed for his son Edward Dee, who he said had come from New Zealand to help him because of the shortage of labour. He had 120 acres of hay to get in and 80 acres of corn and had not sufficient labour to keep the thistles down.
>
> *Worcester Herald*, 8 July 1916

As Mr Dee's testimony indicates, a labourer's work was not merely about the planting and harvesting of produce; maintenance was also required to keep thistles down, lime trees, clear ditches and deal with pests.

SHOT-BORER BEETLE AND FRUIT TREES

> The Royal Agricultural Society's expert zoologist Mr C. Warburton visited Evesham to investigate injury done to fruit trees by the shot-borer beetle pest … He said that he had found two distinct kinds of beetles [and] suggested placing oak stakes in the ground to trap the beetles and a spraying or painting making the trees as undesirable for the beetle as possible.
>
> *Birmingham Daily Post*, 17 August 1917

Tractors and mechanization

One suggested solution to the shortage was the adoption of more efficient machinery, a strategy advocated by the newly appointed County War Agricultural Committee in late 1915. Growers in Pershore and the Vale already had a predisposition towards mechanization, where they could afford it. Threshing machines worked well on the flat lands around Pinvin and Throckmorton, and, in early 1914, newspapers as far away as Otautau, New Zealand, noted that:

> Mr Wyles of Evesham had designed a new small motor plough to work between fruit trees, with a cost of £50 [£2,200 today] it was not going to be utilized by many. The lucky few who could hire or own such a contraption benefited from its ability to plough at a speed of three miles an hour … over an acre a day on three gallons of petrol.
>
> *Otautau Standard and Wallace Country Chronicle*, 17 February 1914

The Humphries family of Pershore had opened the 'new' Atlas Works beside the station in 1883, where they manufactured the mechanical equipment needed by farmers in the locality and beyond, but it was not cheap. Once again using the co-operative principle, Pershore growers banded together to purchase agricultural machinery. St Andrew's Parish Council purchased potato sprayers to hire out to smallholders and allotment keepers, storing the machines at the fire station on Bridge Street. At the end of December 1915, the *Birmingham Daily Post* reported that in 'Pinvin near Pershore, the local Agricultural Co-operative Society has subscribed over two thirds of the cost of a motor plough for the use of small-holders who are members of the society.'

The following year, the success of the Pinvin scheme was reported in newspapers across the country:

Ploughing with a motor tractor near Pershore. (Berrow's Worcestershire Journal, *1915)*

CO-OPERATIVE USE OF MOTOR PLOUGH

With the growing scarcity of labour, it is important to make the most effective use of all available labour-saving implements and machines. A good example of what can be done in the way of purchasing implements on the co-operative principle is afforded by the Society formed at Pinvin in Worcestershire. The estimate was that the expenses for the first year would be £181 5s, which included repayment of principal and interest at five percent for eight years, wages of a man part time, petrol, repairs, etc., sundry expenses and a balance for reserve and contingencies.

The estimated receipts were as follows: Ploughing two hundred acres at 15s per acre, £150, skimming 150 acres at 2s 6d per acre, £18 15s, and scruffing fifty acres, at 5s, £12 10s, which would have made the accounts balance. The sum of £92 10s was raised by subscription, and £90 from friends of the movement, the latter sum being treated as a loan share capital. After paying for the plough, a stock of petrol and for certain labour in preliminary trials there was an adverse balance of £2 11s 9d. The plough was not obtained in time for the autumn ploughing in 1915, and in the early part of 1916 the weather was too bad to allow it to be used very much. From the work carried out, however, the members were satisfied that the enterprise will be both successful and profitable.

Whitby Gazette, 30 June 1916

However helpful the machinery might be to farmers, it was manual labour that was needed to produce enough food to feed both the nation and the armed services; and in Pershore and the Vale, help came from many sources, as the following chapter reveals.

NOTES

1   For further discussion of agriculture in the twentieth century see A. Howkins, *Reshaping Rural England: A Social History 1850–1925* (London: Routledge, 1991) and A. Howkins, *The Death of Rural England: A Social History of the Countryside Since 1900* (London: Routledge, 2003).
2   R.C. Gaut, *A History of Worcestershire Agriculture and Rural Evolution* (Worcester: Littlebury Press, 1939).
3   *Birmingham Daily Post*, May and June 1914.
4   M. Bramford, *Voices from the Past: Pershore 1900–1935* (Malvern: Aspect Design, 2015).

3

WHO IS BRINGING IN THE HARVEST?

Pershore Heritage and History Society and University of Worcester History Students

⁂

The growers of Pershore found it increasingly difficult to recruit sufficient appropriately skilled labour in wartime to prepare the land, nurture the crops and harvest the fruit and vegetables required to feed the nation. Consequently, they began to employ a surprising number of different groups of people, particularly on the larger properties. One farmer explained to a military tribunal in 1916 that:

> He farmed 263 acres, 177 [of which were] arable and also some 16 acres of orchard at Quinton. His pre-war staff was nine regular men, now he only had a carter, a cowman and a general hand. He employed seven local women and expected nine University ladies shortly. He had been obliged to sacrifice seven acres of bush land in consequence of labour shortage. He had, as a farmer, done as required, planted as much wheat as possible and his crop had yielded 43 bushels to ten acres. He challenged any farmer to beat that …
>
> *Worcester Herald*, 1 July 1916

Over the course of the war, the workforce included Irish labourers, gypsies and Birmingham factory workers who traditionally headed to Worcestershire to help with the summer harvests, augmented by local women, children and men too old to fight, Boy Scouts, school pupils, university students, Belgian refugees, and eventually in some areas, German prisoners of war.

The harvest of 1914 was well on the way when war was declared in early August, and the initial burst of volunteer enthusiasm ensured that it was collected on time. The most worrying concerns that the following year's harvest would suffer because of labour shortages were largely unfounded because of the efforts of local people, students and Boy Scouts. Age was no restriction, indeed on 12 June 1915, a recommendation was received by the Worcestershire Chamber of Agriculture that facilities be afforded to old age pensioners to help in farm operations. The *Worcester Herald* noted on 1 August 1915 that, 'The market gardeners in the district are finding the help given them by the Boy Scouts from various towns, and ladies who have come from Birmingham University, London and other places, very valuable'. *The Birmingham Evening Post* had already reported on 21 June 1915 that, 'Female labour has been introduced in all branches of farming work,' but the supply was 'altogether inadequate to meet the demand.'

From the summer of 1915 onwards, female students at Birmingham University volunteered to work on the farms of Pershore and the surrounding villages. Some camped, others were housed in barns, whilst the parish council in Wick rented cottages for the women who arrived to pick hops in September 1916. The students wrote about their experiences for the university's magazine, *The Mermaid*:

National Service poster requesting 10,000 women for farm work. (Pershore Heritage Centre)

FIELD WORK AT ELMLEY CASTLE

The party which set out for work was a strange sight to see; our attire was a marvellous motley – old waterproofs, mackintosh skirts, hockey leggings, old hats, bathing caps, sun-bonnets, motor-coats, hurden aprons – anything old which would keep out the wet. One enterprising lady wore her father's boots over her own. We were usually laden with sacks and buckets to pick into, baskets of bread and cheese, and bottles of water. Our bedraggled appearance on our return home after a wet day was even more entertaining, and proved a festival for the village children.

Our work was of various kinds: pea-picking, bean-picking, plum-picking, thistle-cutting, bean-topping and for the last week, harvest work. Plum-picking proves exciting at times, when two ladders locked together over a tree begin to slip, and the pickers clasp hands in terror, gazing with agony into each other's eyes, waiting for the end … it was back-breaking work, and three weeks of it seems now impossible to contemplate. At the end of our last day's bean-picking one of the party solemnly plucked a bean-flower, and ground it into the earth with her heel, as a declaration of our heartfelt detestation of dwarf kidney-beans. Harvest-work was the heaviest, but by far the most interesting of all the kinds of work we tried. Largely because we felt it to be more vitally important than the other work, we were, one and all, extremely enthusiastic over it …

The Mermaid, 1915–16, pp. 23–4. By kind permission of the
Cadbury Research Library, Birmingham University

The students' hard work and patriotic approach was praised in the local newspapers:

There are also a large number of young ladies from Birmingham University and other young ladies of high social position working for various growers around the district in gathering produce. The only remuneration that they ask is that they are paid the same as is usually paid for unskilled labour, and out of this they deduct sufficient for their maintenance and travelling expenses. The remainder they are giving to various charitable organisations in connection with the war.

Worcester Herald, 31 July 1915

In 1915 the yield of plums in the Vale of Evesham was heavy and the *Worcester Herald*, on 27 September 1915, claimed that: 'many men have been able to earn as much as £4 a week plum picking, and there have been cases where men have made £5.' The traveller community traditionally helped with the harvests in the area and were one group of skilled workers able to achieve such high wages. Students, travellers, and volunteers arrived in the summer months, and for some a trip to the Vale formed their summer holiday.

William Haynes and other navvies near Pershore before the war. (Nancy Fletcher)

By the summer of 1915, married women were being strongly encouraged to contribute to the harvesting and an article in the *Worcester Herald* praised a married woman, who, being 'too delicate for farm work of any sort', had established at her cottage a form of miniature crèche, minding the children of women who took on outdoor work such as weeding, hoeing, and raking. The degree to which agricultural work beyond the family smallholding or market garden was incompatible with domestic responsibilities quickly became an issue and concern was expressed about the welfare of children if their mothers worked. Some mothers were criticized for their reluctance to leave their children, others for being too willing to do so.

However, in the winter months, when many of these groups were not available, there was once again a shortage of labour:

THE PROBLEM ON FARM AND GARDEN

The Labour difficulty is the problem of the day both in garden and farm … In some parishes more women are working on the gardens and farms than is usual in the winter, but many women who work on the land in the summer are not inclined to face the discomforts of winter work. In many cases they are receiving allowances, which make them practically independent …

If women were provided with stout boots or clogs and equipped so that they could face the discomforts and unpleasantness of winter work on the land without the prospect of wet feet, and consequent colds, there would be probably many more ready to work. The initial expense of adequately equipping themselves prevents the offer of their service in many instances. Without the services of more women and boys in the future it is difficult to see how the necessary work will be done.

Birmingham Daily Post, 30 December 1915

Farmers continued to find it difficult to get skilled stockmen, shepherds and milkmen and, in September 1915, an official statement was made that skilled agricultural labourers were to be 'starred' and not canvassed for recruiting. Women were trained in dairy-work, feeding calves and young stock and even provided with classes in weeding and clearing undergrowth, but Pershore farmers still refused to accept an easy solution:

WHY SHOULD NOT WOMEN MILK COWS?

There is a difference of opinion as to the ability and the inclination of women to milk cows. At a recent meeting at Pershore, Mr J. W. Dee, farmer, declared that it was impossible to entrust women with the management and milking of a herd of cows, and other farmers said there was strong feeling against employing women in milking. In some villages, they declared, there is not a woman who can milk.

Women still do much of the milking in Scotland and Wales, and in some parts of England (says a correspondent), and there seems no reason why they should not do this work in the Midlands if this would be of real assistance to the farmers in the difficult times before them.

Coventry Standard, 25 February 1916

On 9 November 1916 the Pershore sub-committee of the County War Agricultural Committee argued that skilled agricultural labourers should be banned from enlisting in the armed forces[1] and, indeed, military tribunals in 1916 exempted many skilled workers like Edward Milward:

Edward John Milward (26, single), a butcher and market gardener, said that he was the only one left to manage the business. His brother had joined the Army and his mother was an invalid. He had a boy at the shop and a man on the garden of four acres. He killed a beast, and six sheep and a pig (in season) per week. In addition he had 30 acres of pasture land, four horses, five cattle and seven pigs. In reply to Mr Davis, he said that if he had to go both businesses would have to be given up. His late father had had the land for about 50 years. Conditional exemption granted.

Worcester Herald, 30 September 1916

Conscientious objectors could have been a possible source of labour, but they were few in number, farmers were reluctant to employ them, and military tribunals less than sympathetic to their beliefs.[2] In July 1916, 28-year-old Maurice Knaggs, a labourer working for a fruit grower in Throckmorton near Pershore, was called before a military tribunal. He explained that,

> His objection arose from his belief that war involved the surrender of the Christian ideal, and was a denial of human brotherhood. He formally became a member of the Society of Friends early this year, after having been an adherent since May 1914. Prior to this he was a Congregationist.
>
> *Worcester Herald*, 22 July 1916

The tribunal was keen to ascertain what sacrifices he had made for his belief. Maurice replied that he had given up a well-paid job in an audit department to work on the land, undertaken first aid work and helped with victims of bombing in London, but had given up medical work as he was opposed to inoculation schemes. His application to remain on the land was unsuccessful: the tribunal sent him off for non-combatant service.

Those presiding over the military tribunals seemed to give only spasmodic consideration to the significant necessity for men to be spared military service because of the needs of agriculture. The *Worcester Herald* reported on 1 July 1916 that a farmer with 44 acres showed the tribunal panel a letter from the Board of Agriculture supporting his application for military exemption, only to be told that the Board had no jurisdiction over the tribunal. Women were identified to fill the vacancy and, on 1 May 1916, the *Birmingham Evening Post* reported that the National Land Council, which had already deployed about 4,000 women, was sending 100 more to the area for the strawberry, raspberry, gooseberry and plum harvests. They were joined once more by Birmingham University students:

STRAWBERRY PICKERS DIARY

> Now that the lapse of time has blurred their original clear outlines, memories of camp at first present themselves as a confused series of ideas – tents, strawberries, rain, 'count your blessings,' the motor lorry, baked potatoes, and more rain – the whole pervaded by a thrilling sense of freedom from restraint, and general well-being.
>
> Then, as clearer vision rises, comes the remembrance of the early morn, when one passed from a dream of strawberries which grew in weird and wonderful geometric designs, to the consciousness that there was a terrific hubbub somewhere, and a voice from afar dispelled the fast-vanishing dream. 'Half past-three! Time to get up!' At the same time the half-open tent flap permitted a view

of a maiden whose toilet had been performed with more regard for haste than elegance, and who, by the vigorous application of a tent peg to the frying-pan, seemed determined to allow nobody to slip back into sleep …

Now began the labours of the day, with their attendant joys and woes. Usually the first hours were devoted to gathering raspberries, an occupation which involved free shower baths if there had been rain or heavy dew during the night. This inconvenience, however, was easily remedied, as the rest of the day was spent among 'strawberries,' under the full rays of the sun …

To pass over the hours spent on the strawberry fields, since they bore too close a resemblance to work to provide entirely happy memories – imagine how we straggled back to camp in twos and threes, along a winding lane that ran uphill all the way. Imagine with what relief we rounded the corner of the hedge, and made straight for our own particular tent. Imagine too, the joy with which the gong was heralded – surely that old frying-pan never had a more joyous ring than at dinner-time! – and the heterogeneous mob which sat down to dinner! And dinner itself – no feast of epicure or gourmand was ever more appreciated than Mrs Walpole's Irish stew and baked potatoes …

In this way day followed day, now with sunshine, now rain, but always filling us with that health of body which goes far in promoting a healthy outlook upon life …

'Field Work in Elmley Castle' in *The Mermaid*, 1915–16, pp. 21–3. By kind permission of the Cadbury Research Library, Birmingham University

At the end of 1916, the Pershore County War Agricultural Sub-Committee reported that it had deployed 832 women and eighty-seven farmers across the Pershore district.

Lance Corporal Will Haynes and his family in 1916. (Nancy Fletcher)

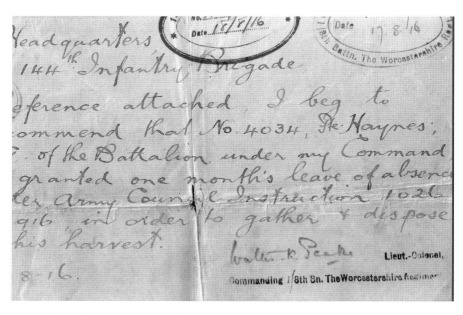

Request for Will Haynes to be given leave to help with the harvest. (Nancy Fletcher)

Convalescing soldiers, or those in training locally, often helped with the harvest and in August 1916, William George Haynes of Newlands was granted permission to take leave from active service at the Front and return home to help with the harvest.

On returning to the Front he continued to write home to his wife.

Dec 10/16

L/Cpl Haynes WG
B Company
1/8 Worcesters
B. E. F.

Dear Nell

Just a line to let you know that I received yours letter quite safe Dear Nell send me a good parcel for Xams as I shall be out of the trenches for Xams Dear Nell I have not seen Victor at all but I have seen Len Rose and Jack Coombe again all the Old boys have join us again I mean them that was gassed Dear Nell don't write me a letter like that last one because I am alright at present and in the best of health I have only got a little cold but we have had a lot of rain this last day ore two we are going up to the trenches today for the last time before Xams so send me a good parcel for Xmas and send im on the 16 of this month and then I shall get im on Xmas day now don't forget I am glad to here that you are looking after the pigeons alright and I hope you let them out for a fly now and again so I think this is all as I cant stop to write any more at present I remain yours loving Husband W G Haynes

Kisses for the Children xxxxxxxxxxxxxxx and one for yourself xxxxxxxxxxxxxxx

Lilly liked that letter that I wrote to her
just remember me to all at home and to Old tack

So, By By for the present

William was killed before the parcel arrived, leaving his wife a widow with four children.

The authorities' decision to send William home during the Battle of the Somme was an indication of how important food had become to the war. The deployment of women to work on the land was formalised in 1917, nationally by the establishment of the Women's Land Army,[3] and locally by the creation of a labour agency in the Vale, suggested by the indefatigable Geoffrey F. Hooper, which answered the needs of farmers requiring labour and women wanting work.

Able-bodied men doing vital jobs, such as roadworks, which prevented them being conscripted into the forces, were strongly encouraged to give part-time

Will Haynes' widow Nell, her three children and visitors outside their cottage in Newlands, Pershore. (Nancy Fletcher)

Land Army girls. (Berrow's Worcester Journal, *8 March 1918*)

help to farmers during haymaking and harvest-time. William George Marshall, the 36-year-old gamekeeper to the 1,500-acre Bishampton Estate, was given exemption from military service in 1917 on condition that he remained in this employment and continued to assist farms and allotment holders in the neighborhood. Again in 1917, women students of Birmingham University returned to the area:

ELMLEY CASTLE

Looking back on six weeks of war-work at Elmley Castle, our memories seem too bounded – and blurred – by vistas and vistas of green. What? – you ask. Green peas! For we picked peas of all varieties and peas in all directions – in Elmley itself, at Fladbury, Cropthorne, Wick, and Evesham. Those of you whose experience of picking peas is confined to the leisurely gathering of a few pounds from the kitchen garden can scarcely imagine a long day's work in a field of peas where the plants are only about a foot high and weight is reckoned in pots of 40lbs.

After long monotonous days of picking, often under a blazing sun, one becomes strangely like an automaton, a machine adjusted to root up plants and pick off pods and move on at certain intervals. You forget that there are such things as skies and clouds, trees and flowers, above and around you; the memory of people and of towns is buried in some far-distant past; you forget to think and to feel, and just go on picking either until you suddenly discover that you are desperately hungry or until work stops …

Only once did we have time to see how truly picturesque was the field in which we were working. On the last day of all, two of us did 'day work', pulling seed-peas and hoeing. Day work is much less strenuous than piece-work, and … We enjoyed that last day partly because we got to know the 'regular' women really well, for we joined them in building up a huge camp fire, whose smoke made the boughs of the giant tree above dance riotously, and also because the wide twenty-acre field was a glorious medley of colour …

The Mermaid, 1916–17, pp. 21–3. By kind permission of the
Cadbury Research Library, Birmingham University

There were concerns that under-taking arduous work on the land would compromise young girls' femininity; something that advertisers of cosmetic products addressed.

Local girls also worked on their parents' and neighbouring farms but life on the land was not idyllic or quaint; it was often cold, wet and arduous and in some instances dangerous:

*A wartime advert for Royal Vinolia hand cream. (*Hull Daily Mail*, 27 September 1917)*

GIRL FARM WORKER SCALPED

Mr G.H.T. Foster, coroner, held an inquest at Evesham as to the death of Ivy May Bayliss (16) daughter of Mr F. Bayliss, market gardener at Murcott, who died in Evesham hospital, following an accident. She was employed as a farm worker at Murcott by Mr W.A. Fisher, of Evesham, and on October 9 she was at work crushing cake, and went to put some flour on a slack driving belt, when her hair caught in the spindle and she was shockingly injured before the machinery could be stopped, and she died on November 20.

Gloucester Echo, 25 November 1918

German POWs

At the end of 1916, the government began to employ German prisoners of war to help with agriculture in the Evesham Vale:

The district provides peculiar scope for the experiment of using German prisoners, who it is proposed, should work in gangs of 20 under the supervision of a competent working overseer, himself a market gardener.

It will not be sufficient to arrange for small parties of prisoners to be made available for work on the farms. The farmers must be persuaded to employ the prisoners. For many months past skilled agricultural workers of nominally enemy alien nationality have been at the disposal of agriculturalists who wished to employ them, but very few have left the internment camps for the land.

Yorkshire Evening Post, 23 November 1916

In 1917 after an inspection of potential premises in Bowbrook in Peopleton, a camp was established and in August a large crowd assembled at Pershore station to see the arrival of fifty German prisoners:

… who have been sent by the Government to work on the land in the Peopleton district, mainly through the representation of two prominent growers Messrs F.R. Pearson of Peopleton and L. Oakes, Seaford Grange, Bow Brook House… They will be under the supervision of Lieut. C Witbern, a guard of 15 men and a sergeant.

They arrived on a special train from Dorchester and were the object of keen curiosity. Not a single remark was made by one of the crowd to the prisoners whose appearance however was much commented on as offering a striking comparison to the English guard accompanying them.

The British Tommies, who someone dubbed 'the Old Sweats' were big manly fellows whereas the prisoners were with the exception of two or three, all undersized, whose ages were difficult to gauge. One spoke English fluently and conspicuous on his breast wore the Iron Cross. Asked if they were recent prisoners, the Captain, who came as far as the station with them, announced they were captured about a month earlier.

Worcester Herald, 4 August 1917

A further sixty-five prisoners were accommodated at the workhouse and the work carried out by the Germans was hard, but of great value to the over-stretched farmers and smallholders, as the following article demonstrates:

PRISONERS ON THE LAND

There are eighty prisoners in Evesham, and more are wanted. The correspondent describes meeting them leaving work, 'alert and smiling, fork over shoulder, with the content that a day's work on Mother Earth gives to those who love her ...'

One of the largest fruit growers in the district said that the prisoners ... were selected men, all knowing something of the soil, and one being the owner of a big market garden at Hamburg. They work eight hours a day, with two hours' break at midday. The employers pay 4d an hour, of which the men get a penny, the balance going to the War Office. They are well fed and well housed ...

I was shown ... an array of hundreds upon hundreds of 'handlights' protecting the early vegetables from the weather's inclemency. These had all been placed in position in their thirty symmetrical lines by the smiling men who passed us. My companion lifted one, and showed me verdant early cauliflowers planted by one of the prisoners. Under a 'rim-glass' by its side was early vegetable marrow ... Another part had been dug by the prisoners for carrot and turnip. In yet another there had been preparation for the planting of potatoes. The man who showed these things urged the further employment of the expedient with all the force at his command.

Chelmsford Chronicle, 30 March 1917

Despite this positive endorsement of the scheme, the employment of German prisoners of war was not a straightforward affair; providing sufficient guards could be labour-intensive and older soldiers were sometimes given this task. In time, guards became more relaxed; prisoners were accompanied to and from farms only, and trusted to work without military supervision. Rumour surrounded the German POWs and the response of the locals to them, which was sometimes considered too friendly:

Col. Wheeler said he thought that the way in which the German Prisoners were being treated by young girls and other people throughout the country by waving to and communicating with them showed that people did not realise how our prisoners were being treated ... With regard to the farmers giving them cider and cigarettes in the early days, a case was reported where a famer had given the men cider and was warned that such a thing could not be allowed ...

Dr Martin said that in the Evesham district cases had come to his knowledge of young girls waving their hands, making overtures to the prisoners and giving them cigarettes.

Evesham Journal, 4 April 1918

Others regarded the POWs with deep suspicion, and stirred up trouble:

GERMAN PRISONERS SPOIL POTATO SEED AT EVESHAM

A remarkable instance of German trickery was furnished by a ... letter from ... a market gardener from Evesham, who had engaged a number of German prisoners to cultivate his land, the majority of his men having joined the army. He had, he says, discovered Germans engaged in planting potatoes deliberately removing the eyes of the tubers before putting them in the drills, thus rendering the seed absolutely useless.

Birmingham Mail, 26 April 1917

The story was reported in the national press, prompting local farmers to investigate:

AN EVESHAM SCARE

At a meeting of the Worcestershire Food Production Committee on Saturday, it was stated that an investigation had been made into the allegation that German prisoners had cut the eyes out of seed potatoes when they planted them.

The Evesham Sub-committee has gone into the matter, and the potatoes planted (only a small quantity) had been uncovered and were found to be perfect.

Birmingham Evening Post, 30 April 1917

Further inquiries were made to uncover the rumour's source, which suggests a strong sense of justice, and the Welsh journalists responsible were prosecuted and fined under the Defence of the Realm Act.

Despite their hard work, by 1918 a war-weary population had become irritated by feeding and paying German prisoners and there were objections when the men received a pay rise for helping to lift potatoes and participate in harvesting. At a meeting of the Pershore Farmers' Union, Mr Deakin protested:

The authorities seemed to think that the farmer was an orange to be sucked dry. He would pay any price for British labour rather than agree to the increase for Germans, who were the greatest thieves he had come in contact with.

Worcester Herald, 7 September 1918

The Chairman of Pershore National Farmers Union agreed, 'His experience being that the German labour was the dearest form of labour he had ever employed.'

Whilst all of these workers strove to produce food on the farms and market gardens, the nation was encouraged to increase the domestic production of food on allotments, in cottage gardens, even in buckets and window boxes. Again, women found this work was added to their already heavy domestic burden, and it was suggested in 1917 that:

Probably there is no woman who leads a more cramped, unattractive life than the countrywoman … But the countrywoman has become a very valuable asset to the nation. But for her, in many villages throughout the country, there would be no one to care for the gardens and allotments.

Coventry Evening Standard, 11 August 1917

NOTES

1 Worcestershire County War Agricultural Committee Minutes, Worcestershire Archives and Archaeological Service (WAAS): Accession no. 179. Reference no. 259.9:2. Parcel: 4.
2 For a more detailed exploration of the treatment of conscientious objectors see L.S. Bibbings, *Telling Tales About Men: Conceptions of Conscientious Objectors to Military Service During the First World War* (Manchester: MUP, 2009).
3 For a more in-depth discussion of the Land Army see B. White, *The Women's Land Army in First World War Britain* (Basingstoke: Palgrave MacMillan, 2014).
4 WAAS: Accession no. 179. Reference no. 259.9:2. Parcel: 5 (i).

4

HOW WOMEN KEPT THE HOME FIRES BURNING

The Pershore Women's Institute

Wartime brought many challenges to the domestic lives of the women of Pershore, who struggled to feed their families and maintain their homes on limited budgets in an era of food shortages and rising prices. During the latter years of the nineteenth century, there had been a flurry of affordable advice manuals on the market, like *Mrs Beeton's Household Management* and Cassells' *Household Guide*. This was as nothing to the deluge of advice women received about efficient living and prudent housewifery immediately following the declaration of war and in the years that followed.[1]

Challenges and changes for women in wartime

In the early days of the conflict, women were encouraged not to panic and food hoarding was discouraged, yet on the day war was declared some shops were forced to shut as they ran out of goods. The *Evesham Journal* pointed out on 8 August 1914 that a woman, 'buying in large quantities in advance, is burdening her sisters with needlessly high prices', but such guidance was not always heeded, even when food hoarding was made a crime. The wives and families of servicemen were reassured that they would be financially provided for when their husbands were away at war. The government introduced separation allowances whereby a fixed portion of a servicemen's wages was paid directly to their wives or mothers, supplemented by an allowance for each child. Some women were better off; many others were not and found making ends meet challenging, particularly those referred to as 'unmarried wives' who had no right to financial support.

Advert for Sunlight Soap. (Essex Newsman, 21 August 1915)

THE MOTHER IN WAR TIME

"We are fighting for our liberty . . . and for the Virtue and Honour of our Womanhood and our innate love of home."
—Mr. W. CROOKS, M.P.

MOTHERS will take courage from the words of Mr. Will Crooks. That inborn love of Home· of which he speaks is begotten of perfect Motherhood.   Although we lay stress upon the purity and efficiency of

SUNLIGHT SOAP

we always make our claims secondary to the needs of those we serve. No soap can be too good for the Wives, Mothers, and the homes of our gallant Sailors and Soldiers.

£1,000 Guarantee of Purity on every Bar.

The name Lever on Soap is a Guarantee of Purity and Excellence.
LEVER BROTHERS LIMITED, PORT SUNLIGHT.

It was assumed that women created and maintained a home for men's benefit. Thus in October 1914, Pershore Rural District Council decided that it would not build sixteen houses planned for Pinvin as they would not be wanted by young men who had gone to fight and might not return. There was no suggestion that a woman or fatherless family might need to be housed; it was expected that others in their family would take them in or that they would turn to the workhouse. War put a stop to further housing and planned utilities; on 21 October 1914 the *Gloucester Echo* reported the cessation of schemes to improve the water supply in Pershore and develop twenty-four cottages in Littleton.

The health of working–class families was precarious in 1914, threatened by illness, disease and accident. Death was not reserved for men on the Front: as many as one-fifth of children died before reaching the age of 5. Alongside the lists of those who fell in conflict, newspapers regularly reported incidences of scarlet fever, diphtheria, German measles and tuberculosis. During the four years of the war, thirty-two children were buried in Pershore cemetery. The outbreak of hostilities in August 1914 were overshadowed by personal loss for one extended family in Wick, whose young child died as a result of drinking scalding hot water from a kettle, according to a report in the *Worcester Herald* on 1 August 1914.

Working–class women, particularly if unmarried, continued to undertake employment, play a role in family businesses, or take in sewing or washing at home in wartime. If husbands, sons or male employees joined the services, women were obliged to take on new tasks and roles in shops, businesses or farms. Many women worked in market gardens with their husbands or sons, who might also

Pershore Terrace, Pinvin. (Cynthia Johnson)

have other employment: both the census of 1911 and the *Pershore Fruit Growers Register 1915* list as 'orchard-owners', 'fruit-growers' or 'market gardeners' men who also were publicans, wheelwrights and grocers. The harvesting, marketing and preservation of fruit and vegetables on these comparatively small properties would, at intermittent points of time, have needed the efforts of husbands, wives and children. It is therefore easy to see how, for these women, domestic and agricultural labour were intertwined; once husbands or sons left for war, women had little choice but to take on more of the outside work as well as the seasonal paid work in the larger orchards and market gardens that they and children had always done in the summer months.

For some women, however, the conflict led to unemployment.[2] A drive to economy in wealthier households made some domestic servants redundant, whilst the National War Savings Committee promoted the idea that 'to dress extravagantly in wartime was unpatriotic' and discouraged women from spending money on 'fripperies'. The consequent downturn in sales of ladies' clothing caused unemployment in the dressmaking, millinery and glove-making trades, a form of work traditionally undertaken by Pershore women in their homes. A charity was quickly established to provide such women with work:

WOMEN'S WORK FUND

Lord Coventry presided at a meeting at Worcester Guildhall yesterday to organise a county committee, with subordinate local committees throughout the city and county, for carrying out the work of the Queen's 'Work for Women' Fund, which has as its object the provision of employment for women who have been thrown out of work by the war …

Various schemes for employment were discussed, and it was decided to divide the county into the same districts as those employed by the Soldiers' and Sailors' Families Association, ladies being appointed to form committees.

Birmingham Daily Gazette, 7 October 1914

Worcestershire established a county committee in October 1914, and the *Worcester Herald* reported on 11 September 1915 that the charity had set up a women's work depot in Pershore.

Other women took more drastic action to deal with unemployment. Despite the dangers of oceanic travel, adverts continued to appear inviting women to emigrate and to take up positions in households in Australia, New Zealand and Canada:

Sir,—May I on behalf of the British Women's Emigration Association, draw the attention of your numerous readers to the very generous offer made by Australia to girls and young women who are willing to go out there as domestic servants?

New South Wales will accept inexperienced girls for domestic service between the ages of 18 and 25; the cost of their passage is only £3 … Experienced servants are accepted up to the age of 55, their passage is £6 paid in advance, and £1 deposit which is returned after the immigrant has entered employment satisfactory to the Immigration Board …

Widows under 35, willing to undertake domestic service, are accepted on the same terms as other servants in New South Wales and Victoria. Widows of soldiers or sailors killed in the war, who are under 35, and have not more than two children, are taken for £3. The fare for their children is £4, for those under 12 and one child taken under three is free … Widows must produce their husband's death certificate, and their own birth certificate if over 30 …

The Queen's Work for Women Fund is ready to assist those eligible for these passages with an outfit made in the Queen's workrooms, and a grant of £2 of which £1 pays the deposit on the fare and £1 is given on arrival as landing money. Application for these benefits must be made through the British Women's Emigration Association …

In these difficult times, when we are obliged to keep workrooms open under the Distress Committee, and supported by other agencies, in order to give employment to women thrown out of work through the war, the generous offer of these Australian States, and of the Queen's Work for Women Fund, should not fail to find some response …

Yours, &c.

EDITH BRIGHT (Mrs Allan H. Bright). Convener, Emigration and Immigration Sectional Committee, National Union of Women Workers.

Liverpool Daily Post, 10 March 1915

Local newspapers advertising emigration passage, 1915.

For middle-class women paid work, particularly once they were married, was neither a necessity nor seen as desirable. They busied themselves with a plethora of voluntary work, fund-raising, knitting, or, in more extreme circumstances, signing up for civil defence work.

Feeding the family

Initial panic buying was replaced by price rises, shortages and strong encouragement to consume less food. Those on the home front were encouraged to grow fruit and vegetables in their gardens; so prolific were citizens' efforts that it was estimated that cottage gardens were responsible for producing some 2.23 billion out of a total of 48.49 billion calories consumed annually in wartime.[3] Hedgerows and common land also provided a source of food 'for free' such as blackberries, damsons and rosehips, although some families went a little further in their desire to feed the family. In September 1914 the *Worcester Herald* reported that a labourer in Pershore was summoned for poaching rabbits and fined 10s (roughly £22 today). Whether poached, kept in the garden, caught or bought legally, rabbits were a staple food for many and could be prepared in a multitude of ways, as roasts, stews, soups or even baked:

BAKED RABBIT

Spread a baking-sheet or tin rather thickly with dripping, At the bottom place a good layer of slices of potato and on top a few thin slices of onion, seasoning well. Arrange pieces of rabbit compactly, add a little bacon or pickled pork in small pieces and season again. Repeat the layers, sprinkle flour, salt, and pepper on the layer of potatoes, and about half fill the dish with hot water. Bake for two hours in a moderate oven, and serve in the dish or arrange the layers as directed in a covered saucepan and cook very slowly by the side of the fire.

Walsall Advertiser, 11 December 1915

By 1915, some foods that had once been common, like flour, eggs and sugar, had become scarce or prohibitively expensive. Eggs were collected and sent to wounded soldiers at home or at the Front; meat and bacon were too expensive for everyday consumption, and newspapers carried adverts to encourage housewives to serve porridge, powdered custard and jellies.

Almost all of the cottages in the district would have had at least one pig to provide bacon and ham for the family, kept in backyards, gardens or orchards. The Pershore and District Pig-Keepers' Association had eighty members in October 1915 and provided a form of insurance for pig owners. All members paid in an agreed amount for each pig they owned and, should their pig die from swine fever or some other disease, the owner would be compensated. In 1915 the association had insured ninety-two pigs and their funds stood at £50. Some women tried to find other ways of avoiding the high prices and provide food for their families.

Adverts for custard powders from Birmingham newspapers, 1917.

Advert for Quaker Oats.
(Manchester Evening News,
30 October 1918)

On 10 July 1915, the *Worcester Herald* reported the case of Mary Jowett, of no fixed abode but who had apparently been coming to the area for many years, who was brought before the magistrates for stealing 5lbs of bacon and six eggs from John Clarke, a butcher in Broad Street. When arrested, Mary pleaded for leniency on the grounds that she had five little children and two sons who had gone to war, one of whom had been killed. Nevertheless, she was convicted and sentenced to one month's imprisonment with hard labour.

Advert for Gip pig and poultry feed. (Gloucester Journal, *14 October 1916*)

At Christmastime women were expected not only to look after their families at home but also to care for those at a distance. Newspapers supplied recipes to make plum puddings to be sent to husbands, sons or penpals at the Front or who had been taken prisoner of war. Food products that are still familiar to us today were advertised widely: 'Send your soldier friends a pudding made with ATORA Shredded Beef Suet. Requires no chopping and makes the best puddings and mincemeat. British made and owned.'

XMAS PRESENTS FOR THE FORCES

For the benefit of our lady readers we give them the best recipe we know of for their Christmas Plum Pudding. Take three-quarters of a pound of flour, two heaped teaspoons of BORWICK'S Baking Powder, two ounces of bread crumbs, one and & half pounds of suet, two pounds of raisins, one pound of currants, ten ounces of sugar, two ounces of almonds, one pound of mixed candied peel, salt and spice to taste. Mix the ingredients well together, and add six eggs, well beaten, and three-quarters pint of milk; divide in two, and boil for eight hours.

Gloucester Journal, 28 November 1914

The plums traditionally associated with Christmas Pudding had generally been replaced by dried fruits and peel by the nineteenth century, yet as the conflict progressed, imported raisins and currants became more difficult to obtain. Food writers either suggested novel ways of catering for Christmas, or recommended that home cooks return to using prunes in puddings like Plum Duff, drying the fruit at home:

TO MAKE PRUNES

Pick the fruit which is ripe and sound, and put it on sieves in the sun to soften. Then place in a spent oven for twenty-four hours, take out and shake up and put back in for another twenty-four hours. Continue doing this until the fruit is as you have known the best quality of prunes in a shop. When all are done pack closely in old jam jars and close tightly. Raisins as we all know have given out, and as they come from Turkey and Greece we are not likely to get any more for Christmas pudding. We cannot replace them, as outdoor English grapes are neither sweet enough not rich enough but preserved plums cut in pieces will make an excellent substitute.

Portsmouth Evening News, 8 September 1915

The national shortage of sugar, previously imported from the Austro-Hungarian Empire, meant that cooks needed recipes for making their puddings without sweeteners.

SMALL AND VERY LIGHT PLUM PUDDING

With 3 oz of the crumbs of a stale loaf, finely grated and soaked in quarter of a pint of boiling milk, mix 6 oz of suet minced very small, 1 oz of dry bread crumbs, 10 oz of stoned raisins, a little salt: the grated rind of a lemon and three eggs, leaving out one white. Boil the pudding for three hours and serve with a sweet sauce. Put no sugar in it.

Derbyshire Courier, 9 November 1915

The intensification of naval warfare in 1916 exacerbated food shortages, and, as the food crisis escalated, queuing for food was added to women's other domestic tasks. By 1917 housewives were queuing for up to six hours for a tub of margarine in

Worcester. Initially there were attempts to persuade housewives to economise, and ensure that their families consumed less food, more vegetables, less fat and meat. Food Control Committees were introduced in towns to prevent profiteering and the Defence of the Realm Act forbade householders from throwing away edible food scraps.

The better off were encouraged to eat less bread as it was the staple food of the working classes. Fines were introduced for wasting bread and on 29 May 1917, a proclamation from King George V was read out in all churches, which emphasized the importance of food to the nation's war effort and exhorted citizens to:

> … reduce the consumption of bread in their respective families by at least one-fourth of the quantity consumed in ordinary times … Abstain from the use of flour in pastry and moreover carefully to restrict or wherever possible to abandon the use thereof in all other articles than bread.
>
> The King's Proclamation, 29 May 1917

Newspapers were full of advice to wives and mothers on how to make the most of scraps and to use the ample crop of plums or any jam they had procured. During the harvest season in 1917 readers were reminded that 'Plums are Cheap' and further advised to prepare them in the following way:

> Half fill a pie dish with stoned plums, a sprinkling of sugar, grated nutmeg, and lemon. Cover with tapioca just boiled until it is clear. Bake in a moderate oven and serve hot or cold. Batter may be used instead of tapioca.
>
> *Southern Reporter*, 5 September 1917

War takes its toll

The incessant strain of life on the home front took its toll on family relationships. Generations within a single family each came under seemingly insurmountable pressures to play their part in the war effort. Some widows ran smallholdings with their sons, but this was not always a harmonious experience. Fifty-year-old William Marshall, resident of Wyre Piddle, was summoned for threatening to murder his mother who told the court that:

> He had threatened her during the last fortnight. It was his nasty temper. All she wanted was for her son to live away from her house. When she locked him out he would burst the door open. She wanted him to keep away from her …

William denied the charge and claimed that:

The land was as much his as his mother's and he did not want to be pushed out in a minute. His mother had all his earnings … He had no money.

He was bound over to keep the peace for six months.

Worcester Herald, 1 September 1917

Women struggling to cope in difficult circumstances received limited sympathy or support. Maud Hewiett was a mother of six who lived in Church Street, Pershore; her husband had been injured at the Front and transferred to duties with the Military Foot Police. On 27 October 1917, the *Worcester Herald* published an account of the trial at which she was found guilty of wilfully neglecting two of her children. Both the School Attendance Officer and Dr Mary Williams, Worcestershire's Assistant Medical Officer, found Maud's domestic skills to be wanting. Dr Williams explained that when she had seen the children on 11 September they 'had scabies and were very dirty. The house was not exactly dirty but there was a want of care about it'. In her defence, Maud said that she 'had spent pounds at the chemists in trying to cure the scabies.' Prior to the establishment of the National Health Service in 1948, both visits to the doctor and medicines were expensive, especially for working-class women such as Maud. Unfortunately, the magistrates were of the opinion that, as Maud was in receipt of government separation allowance, she must have more money coming into the house than before the war, and by implication should have been able to afford treatment. Furthermore, the court ascertained that whilst there was nowhere in Pershore where this poor mother could disinfect the children's blankets, the neighboring town of Evesham provided facilities for this. Maud Hewiett, whose weekly separation allowance from the army was £1 17s, was fined 10s. Viscount Deerhurst, the presiding magistrate, told her that in future she must pay more attention to the cleanliness of her house and her children.

By Christmas 1917, both the expense and availability of good meat and fresh ingredients made life very difficult for housewives, even those in a country market town like Pershore. The Food Economy Council provided suggestions for an affordable Christmas dinner, which included French Rice Soup and a main course of stuffed shoulder of mutton, braised celery and baked potatoes followed by fruit pie and custard. The cost of this meal for a family should have cost 4s 5d (approximately £10 today).

Domestic food choices were increasingly restricted and housewives were encouraged to supplement sugar and dried fruits with sweet vegetables, preserves or dried native fruits. Wheat shortages meant that pastry had to be made using ground maize or barley, while oats and potatoes were used in bread and cakes to replace flour and provide much needed bulk. Consequently, the substitution of root vegetables and sweet fruits for sugar meant that when Constance Peel published her *Victory Cookbook* in 1918, the ingredients for her Christmas Pudding resembled nothing so much as an exotic vegetable stew:

WAR CHRISTMAS PUDDING

Materials. — 2oz chopped suet, 4oz apples, chopped and fried in a little fat, the peels of the apples chopped finely, 2oz baked parsnip, 2oz beetroot jam, 2oz currants, 2oz stoned raisins, 1oz dates, 1 lemon (of which the juice is removed to be mixed in the pudding), boiled in water till tender. Pass all the above ingredients through a mincing-machine and add — 1oz ground ginger, 1oz ground cinnamon, 1oz ground clove, 1oz ground nutmeg, a few drops of almond essence, 4oz prepared flour (half rice, half standard). When mixed, put into a greased basin and steam for 4 hours.

Mrs C.S. Peel, *Victory Cookbook*, 1918

PERSHORE RURAL DISTRICT.

THE MEAT (MAXIMUM PRICES) ORDER, 1917.

THE Local Food Control Committee HEREBY GIVE NOTICE that under the Powers conferred upon them by the above Order the Maximum Price of Meat to be sold by Retail in the above District shall, until further notice, be according to the following Schedule, namely :—

SCHEDULE.

BEEF.				s. d.	MUTTON AND LAMB.				s. d.
Sirloin	...	...	...	1 6	Legs ...	...	...	...	1 7
Round, Whole	...	...	...	1 5	Loin, Whole	...	...	...	1 6
,, Joints	...	...	...	1 5½	Shoulder, Whole	...	...	...	1 4
Rump	...	...	...	1 5	,, Half	...	...	...	1 5
Steak, Rump	...	...	...	1 8	Neck, Best End	...	...	...	1 6
,, Round	...	...	...	1 6	,, Middle	...	...	...	1 4
,, Stewing	...	...	...	1 5	,, Thin End	...	...	...	1 0
Flank, Thick	...	...	...	1 5	Breast ...	...	...	...	1 0
,, Thin	...	...	...	1 1	Chops, Loin	...	...	...	1 8
Chine ...	...	...	...	1 6	,, Neck	...	...	...	1 7
Ribs, Flat	...	...	...	1 2	Liver ...	...	...	...	1 2
Brisket, Best End	...	...	...	1 2					
,,	...	...	...	0 11					
Boiling Neck End	...	...	...	0 11	PORK.				
Shin, With Bone	...	...	...	0 8	Pigs' Heads	...	...	...	0 9
,, Without	...	...	...	1 2	Legs, Whole	...	...	...	1 6
Clod of Beef	...	...	...	1 3	,, Half	...	...	...	1 7
Suet ...	...	...	...	1 2	Loins ...	...	...	...	1 6
Kidney	...	...	...	1 4	Neck, Best End	...	...	...	1 6
Liver	...	...	...	1 0	,, Shoulder	...	...	...	1 4
VEAL.					Belly Draft	...	...	...	1 4
Legs	...	...	...	1 4	Breast and Hand	...	...	...	1 4
Fillet	...	...	...	1 7					
Loins	...	...	...	1 6					
Shoulder ...	...	...	...	1 4					
Neck, Best End	...	...	...	1 6					
,, Thin End	...	...	...	0 10					
Breast ...	...	...	...	1 0					
Liver ...	...	...	...	1 3					

The above Prices are for best quality only. Inferior qualities must be charged for at 2½d. per lb. or 20 per cent. profit on fixed price of curcase in every case, whichever is least.

Signed on behalf of the Committee,

H. BASIL HARRISON,

Union Offices, Pershore.

Executive Officer.

8402

Pershore meat prices. (Worcestershire Archives & Archaeological Service)

The government took the bold step of imposing food rationing in January 1918, regulating the sale of meat, fats, sugar and jam, but not bread, still regarded as a dietary staple of the working classes and too important to morale to restrict, despite the fact that its wheat content was tooth-grindingly low.

By this stage, poor supply chains and sharp grocery practices meant that in 1918 a local scandal arose about a shipment of frozen meat from Birmingham which 'was not fit for a dog to eat' and apparently made some of the Pershore residents sick. Magistrates at the Petty Sessions continued to hear cases concerning the small-scale theft of food by men and women. In September 1918, for example, 29-year-old George Edgar Lane and William Thomas Clayton were accused of stealing 12lbs of onions from a field. Onions, which many grew in their gardens and allotments, were a source of flavour in what must increasingly have been rather stodgy and unappealing fare. Cookery writers encouraged their use:

A REALLY CHEAP PIE

Make a dough with a pound and half of flour, three-quarters of a pound of dripping, a teaspoonful of baking powder, and a little water. Grease a pie-dish, roll out the dough, and line the dish. Take the remains of any cold meat: chop it up, season with pepper and salt, a dessert spoonful of chopped onions, a dessert spoonful of chopped parsley, and a few breadcrumbs. Put this mixture into the dish, add a little water or stock, cover the dough, bake and serve with potatoes.

Framlingham Weekly News, 13 January 1917

The emotional pressures of life on the home front were not only caused by economic hardship; war disrupts courtship patterns. At this time, it was not uncommon for working-class courting couples to wait for a pregnancy before they married: community pressure usually prevented either party from scarpering. Conscription, mobilization, and the uncertainties of war sometimes disrupted these customs, and with a transient workforce, there were men whose time in the village was only temporary and who could escape community pressures. It is likely that there is a story of a jilted lover lying behind the following tragedy reported in the summer of 1918:

PERSHORE BABY'S BODY FOUND IN AVON

At the Police Court on Tuesday, Mr H.T. Foster conducted an inquest on the body of a newborn female child, found in the Avon tied up in a bag last Sunday evening … Dr Rusher said the child was quite newly born, but it was in such a bad state of decomposition, having been in the water for fully two months, that he was quite unable to say if the child had had a separate existence, that being so

A mother's meeting at the Mission Hall, Pershore. (Nancy Fletcher)

the Coroner said the Jury could not give a verdict of wilful murder against an unknown person. A verdict of 'Found Dead' was recorded.

Worcester Herald, 13 July 1918

Despite the turmoil and troubles of wartime, many 'soldiered on' with everyday life on the home front. Babies were born and women banded together both formally and informally to give each other support and undertaking all manner of activities to preserve the fruit that was grown, as the following chapter will demonstrate.

NOTES

1 For further discussion of women's experience of the First World War see M. Andrews and J. Lomas (eds), *The Home Front: Images, Myths and Forgotten Experiences* (Basingstoke: Palgrave Macmillan, 2014).
2 For a more in-depth exploration of women and work during the conflict see G. Holloway, *Women and Work in Britain since 1840* (London: Routledge, 2015).
3 T.H. Middleton, *Food Production in War* (Oxford: The Clarendon Press, 1923).

5

PRESERVING FRUIT AND MAKING JAM

Susanne Atkin

᭗᭗᭗

The hard work of farmers and market gardeners to grow fruit and vegetables was only one part of the battle to feed the armed forces and civilian population in wartime. For the fruit and vegetables grown in Pershore's market gardens, allotments, cottage gardens and fruit orchards to be consumed across the country and by troops much further afield at all times of the year, it had to be preserved. Fruit and vegetables needed to be canned, bottled, dried, pulped and preserved in factories and housewives' kitchens; Pershore plums needed to be turned into jam. Prior to the outbreak of war, the working class 'ate much of their fruit as jam'[1]; during the war, jam was a source of calories for all classes. Thus in calculating the rations for active servicemen, who were reckoned to need 3,000 calories a day, each soldier's daily ration included 4oz of jam in 1914. Although this was reduced to 3oz by 1917, throughout the war jam made an important contribution to soldiers' diets. It was quickly noted that:

> There will be certain to be an enormous demand on the part of preserving firms … The Armies and Navies of the world will have to be kept supplied with food and fruit.
>
> *Coventry Evening Telegraph*, 27 May 1915

On the home front, jam continued to have a place in many working-class diets, on bread and also in recipes such as jam roly-poly:

JAM ROLY-POLY PUDDING

6oz of finely chopped beef suet, two breakfast cupfuls of flour, small teaspoonful of salt. Mix to paste, well flour and roll out. Cut paste into two separate rolls.

Spread 2oz jam on one roll evenly all over and roll up that portion. Take white of an egg, whisk it well and spread over other portion; lay previous roll in this. Wring out pudding cloth in boiling water, roll pudding cloth and roll pudding in, and boil for three-quarters of an hour.

Worcester Herald, 31 July 1915

Those who wished to make jam, in factories or homes, were faced with a major problem:

On the outbreak of war, Germany and Austria, on which this country has been dependent for about two-thirds of all the sugar consumed, became suddenly closed as sources of supply. There was imminent danger of a positive famine in sugar, once existing stocks had become exhausted.

Birmingham Daily Post, 2 October 1914

The importance of jam and the shortage of sugar led to increasing government interference in the jam-making industry, whilst housewives explored methods and recipes to preserve fruit with varying degrees of success.

Jam manufacturing

Jam-making in Pershore preceded the outbreak of war. In 1889, the Earl of Coventry instructed John Hill, his land agent, to design and manage a small-scale factory on estate land beside Pershore railway station 'fitting it up in the best modern style'. The *Worcester Chronicle* reported on 30 March 1901 that this gave his tenants 'an opportunity of selling their produce on the spot at fair market prices, thus saving the cost of railway carriage and the various risks attendant upon sending speculative consignments to distant places'. During the mid-1890s, T. W. Beach Co. took over the lease of the Earl's factory; Thomas William Beach was a renowned jam manufacturer from Brentford, Middlesex, who had already leased Lord Sudeley's jam factory at Toddington, Gloucestershire. In 1904, the business was transferred, as the Croome Estate Jam Co., but went into liquidation in 1908. The building was occupied in 1915 by the Huddersfield Fruit Preserving Co.

In May 1889, the newly established Vale of Evesham Fruit Preserving & Pickling Company moved into the old Atlas Works on Pershore High Street (now a garage on the corner with Cherry Orchard), formerly an engineering works operated by Edward Humphries (who had died in 1885). The building was 'skilfully adapted' as a jam factory known as the Pomona Works, and Edward's son E. T. Humphries was a director of the new preserves company. The factory manager was Arthur Beynon, a jam manufacturer from Wales. The company changed its name to the

Croome Estate Jam Co. Ltd letter heading. (Susanne Atkin)

A label for Deakin's jam. (Susanne Atkin)

Vale of Evesham Preserves in 1892. Beynon was recorded as the proprietor of the Pershore Fruit Preserving Factory both in 1899 and during the war.

A jam factory was opened near Evesham railway station in 1899, owned by the Worcestershire Preserving Company; and in 1907, T.W. Beach's company built another on Church Street in Bengeworth. In the same year, William Robert Deakin took over the factory at Toddington in Gloucestershire, which was to be used during the First World War as a canning factory. Deakin was a jam manufacturer from Wigan, Lancashire, who had profited from War Office contracts during the Boer War and in 1906 had moved into Pershore Hall. He increased the acreage of the fruit plantations around the Hall and at Hampton Park in Evesham to supply his Wigan jam factory. During the war, Deakin won government contracts to supply jam and bully beef to the troops. Factories in Pershore and much further afield all contributed to the nationally important role of preserving fruit.

Bruce Bairnsfather cartoon of a soldier eating plum and apple jam. (Susanne Atkin)

THE ETERNAL QUESTION
" When the 'ell is it goin' to be strawberry ? "

Reporting from an army camp 'Somewhere in England', 'Our Territorial Correspondent' for the *Walsall Observer* described 'What Army Rations are like':

For tea we have bread and jam and hot tea. How many varieties and makes of jam I have eaten I have not the slightest idea. Jam is good food, and will do men good; the King said that not long ago when inspecting some of the New Army, so it is so. We have had plum jam, plum and apple, damson, damson and apple, strawberry, raspberry, blackcurrant, greengage, and every other sort of jam that ever was. We have had jam from London, jam from Liverpool, jam from Grimsby, jam from Truro, jam from Australia, and jam from the Lord knows where. We shall be jam experts when we return to civvies. Marmalade also we have had … But for plain tea you can't beat jam.

Walsall Observer, 30 January 1915

French postcard of a catapult for throwing jam-tin bombs into the enemy trenches. (Susanne Atkin)

1914-15... Ancienne catapulte romaine employée actuellement dans les tranchées anglaises
1914-15... Ancient Roman catapult employed actually in the british trenches

Soldiers often found that their rations were not as varied as this report suggests; and the frequent appearance of plum and apple jam was the butt of much satire. Jam had other uses at the Front though – home-made hand grenades were made out of empty jam tins packed with small bits of metal, gravel, gun cotton, a detonator and fuse.

Fruit pulping

The challenges of growing and preserving fruit in the short fruit-picking seasons, and accommodating the shortage of sugar, caused upheaval in the jam industry. The government took control and threatened to commandeer the largest jam manufactories, particularly if it was suspected that the owners were profiteering. The quickest solution to prevent fruit rotting on the trees was to pulp it. This process was cheap, eased railway transport and most importantly, the pulp could be kept and used for jam when sugar supplies or substitutes became available. Pulping was organised in the fruit-growing districts on an industrial scale, as described by the Board of Agriculture and Fisheries:

> It consists in reducing the fruit to a state of pulp by heat, generally by means of steam. The treatment sterilises the fruit, so that it may be kept under suitable conditions without decomposition for an indefinite period. The product is known as fruit pulp. The process can be carried on by any grower who has on his premises an ordinary steam boiler.
>
> *Reading Mercury*, 21 August 1915

According to a harvest report in the *Birmingham Daily Post* on 30 August 1915, 'the yield of plums [this year] has far exceeded all expectations … The railway companies have been for weeks working at high pressure to get the crops away.' The Huddersfield Fruit Preserving Company (who had already acquired Lord Coventry's former jam factory at Pershore station), was 'hard at work pulping plums, and all the jam factories in the country have taken large supplies'. Nevertheless, when Lord Selborne (President of the Board of Agriculture) visited Worcestershire in 1916 he observed:

> … much fruit is wasted, especially in good seasons. The sugar scarcity adds to the difficulty in disposing of the fruit grown. The Sugar Commission is going to try, by arrangement with growers and preservers, to give a sufficient supply of sugar for the whole of the surplus fruit … if the waste of good fruit can be avoided it will be a boon, not only to growers, but to every household. Lord Coventry's suggestion of local pulping places may help to solve the problem of saving fruit.
>
> *Worcester Daily Times*, 17 May 1916

In 1917 the government explained their schemes for pulping and drying, to prevent the waste of surplus food and vegetables:

> After a survey of the chief food-producing areas [the food production] department set about securing suitable premises for conversion into pulping and drying works, realising that if hundreds of thousands of tons of fruit and vegetables can be treated within marked areas … a vast bulk of cheap and nutritious food will be preserved for winter use and a heavy burden removed from the long-distance railway traffic …
>
> To deal immediately with the pulping of plums, centres are already in existence, or will be opened by the end of the month at Bewdley, Pershore, Cheltenham, Harper Adams Agricultural College in Shropshire … Drying centres, so far

established, include Cheltenham and Pershore. At least two other stations will be
opened shortly in Worcestershire.

Manchester Evening News, 11 August 1917

The government identified and equipped suitable premises for the war's duration
and an additional six months, and contracted operating companies to act as agents
for collecting the produce from local growers. On 28 July 1917, the *Birmingham
Daily Post* explained that pulp was stored in 4cwt (203.2kg) barrels, each of which
could 'be filled in five minutes', with 'half-a-dozen pulping vats going at once'.
Owing to the absence of tin, pulping factories were provided with beer barrels
which 'by special processes … were made absolutely sweet receptacles for pulped
fruit'. Barrels made it easier to transport the pulp by rail to the jam factories. The
pulp would be turned into jam when sugar supplies allowed.

The opportunity to make money by setting up a pulping station must have been
irresistible to local entrepreneurs: the government would find and convert the
building, supply the equipment, award a management contract and, six months
after the war's end, the pulping company would be given the opportunity to
buy the building and/or the equipment. The Huddersfield Fruit Preserving Co.
acquired just such a contract. In the town, the Pershore Fruit Growers' Association
purchased the Pomona Works and Central Fruit & Vegetable Market from Arthur
Beynon in July 1917 and set up a new company, Pershore Co-operative Preservers,
'for the purpose of pulping, drying, and canning fruit and vegetables'. At an
Association meeting in Pershore's Masonic Hall the following month, Mr Meades
explained:

> The Association had purchased the property known as the Pomona Works and
> had formed a Co-operative Society, consisting of members of the Association …
> He felt sure this was the finest thing that had come to Pershore, and believed that
> in the future Pershore and prosperity would be synonymous terms.

His colleague Mr Gibbs elaborated:

> For many years the Pershore Association had been anxious to have a pulping
> station … The new factory would tend to make Pershore more and more the
> centre of the district. It would have the capacity to deal with a very large quantity
> of produce … Plant for an improved system of pulping was to be installed,
> and premises erected for vegetable drying. The latter gave promise of being a
> big business, and, what was important to Pershore, it would provide work for
> eighty or a hundred people during the winter months. The plant would have the
> capacity of dealing with about 90 tons of vegetables a week …

Worcester Herald, 4 August 1917

Lucy Conn recalled working at the Pomona factory during the war: 'We dried vegetables, parsnips, and carrots for the troops in the war, and packed them in big cans. They made a lot of pulp from plums that was used to make jam for the troops. The pulp went into barrels.'[2]

A newspaper report in July 1917 refers to five unlisted pulping stations in the Pershore district. As well as the factory by the station and the Pomona Works, there was a pulping station at nearby Upton; another in an outbuilding beside the Crown Inn on Church Street, Eckington; and the Avon Vale Mineral & Cider Making Factory on New Road, Pershore. The pulping station in Eckington was owned by George Welch, a local farmer. The Avon Vale Factory was taken over in June 1917 by the Avon Vale Fruit Pulping & Cider Making Co. The Pershore Medical Officer of Health reported an inspection of a 'new Pulping Factory' in the *Worcester Herald*, 8 September 1917, which was found to be 'dirty', but it is unclear which one.

Fruit pulping was not only carried out in factories; May Byron gave advice in her *Jam Book* on the benefits of making fruit pulp at home:

I would call special attention to the making of fruit pulp. This, if properly prepared, can be used at any time for the basis of jam (inordinate quantities of foreign fruit pulp are imported for that purpose), or for other culinary purposes. It is so cheap, so easy, and so obvious a means of saving fruit, that we have literally no excuse for neglecting it …

Avon Vale Co. trade card from 1916. (Pershore Heritage Centre)

Rub the fruit (having wiped it clean) through a fine sieve, and place the pulp in wide-mouthed bottles which have been thoroughly scalded, dried, and allowed to get quite cold. Cork tightly and cover with a bladder. Place the bottles in a fish-kettle, with cold water up to their shoulders. Let the water heat very gradually till it boils; then let boil for twenty minutes, without cessation. Remove pan from fire, leave bottles in it overnight, and the following day wipe the bottles dry and put them away in a dry place.

Fruit pulp made as above can be kept until it is wanted for any cooking purpose; or it can be made into jam when convenient, as follows: weigh the pulp, place in a pan, and bring to boiling-point; add equal weight of cooked syrup, also boiling. Then boil both together for twenty-five or thirty minutes; this will ensure a better-keeping jam than if sugar were added to the pulp.[3]

Home preservation

Jam making and fruit preservation were strongly encouraged on the home front, since, as a letter to the *Birmingham Post* on 4 September 1915 pointed out: 'The ordinary British matron cannot make munitions or drive tramcars, but she can make excellent jam'. From the outbreak of the war, when housewives were advised how to prevent waste of fruit from the year's heavy crop by bottling correctly, women were bombarded with advice by newspapers and government leaflets about making jam and how to preserve fruit, what ingredients to use, and how to cope with shortages of sugar, glass jars and lids.

CHEAP PLUM JAM

Housewives who are anxious to make plum jam but hesitate to use sugar at its present price, will find that jam made with only 6oz of sugar to 1lb of fruit instead of the usual 1lb, will keep if it is covered with mutton fat after being put in the jars.

Sheffield Evening Telegraph, 18 August 1914

Sugar for making jams and preserves at home became increasingly scarce, as stocks were directed towards production of food for the troops. Substitutes were proposed, such as glucose, but needed to be used with great care:

WARNING TO HOUSEWIVES

Communications have reached the Board of Agriculture and Fisheries referring to a statement which has appeared in the public press to the effect that benzoate of soda may be used to replace sugar in the preparation of jam. The Board are advised that benzoate of soda is quite unsuitable for the purpose in question, and desire to warn the public against its use in jam making. Serious results might follow an attempt to substitute this material for sugar.

Gloucester Journal, 12 August 1916

Some sugar was available, shipped across the Atlantic from Canada. Whilst the preserving factories received priority supplies, in autumn 1917 Pershore witnessed a 'rush for sugar':

The long queues of persons to be seen waiting outside the Pershore Police Station on Wednesday, from 9.30 in the morning till nearly 6 in the evening were beneficiaries under the sugar scheme of the Ladies' War Agricultural Committee of which the Hon. Mary Pakington is the secretary.

Eighty-seven bags of Canadian granulated sugar, weighing approximately four tons, were dispersed to 870 ticket holders in 10lb lots. Supt. Hill, Inspectors Pegg and Greening and Sergt. Drew excellently managed the distribution. Ticket holders came from as far as Bredon and Bredon's Norton, Cropthorne and Charlton, Sutton and Naunton Beauchamp.

Worcester Daily Times, 14 September 1917

Substitutes for sugar were suggested in cookery books and in the newspapers:

A sugar ticket issued by the Food Controller. (Susanne Atkin)

SALT USED AS A SUBSTITUTE FOR SUGAR

How jams can be made with much less sugar than is generally used was shown by Mr William Lawton at the room of the Society of Medical Officers of Health in London.

Ordinarily 1lb of sugar is allowed in jam-making for every pound of fruit. Mr Lawton uses only from three to six ounces of Demerara or soft brown sugar and a varying proportion of salt.

He showed various jams made in this way, including raspberry, gooseberry, plum, greengage, and red and black currant and they tasted well … the experiment can certainly be recommended to housewives who are studying economy. Brilliant in colour, the jams retained the full flavour of the fruit. Indeed the effect of the new method is apparently to give a far richer flavour to the fruit. The only difference in making is that the jams require to be well and slowly boiled, skimming being unnecessary …

It must be admitted (writes another correspondent) that many will not at first care for the distinctly salty taste of some of the jams – gooseberry and raspberry, for instance. The great point is that the abundance of fruit now on the market need not be wasted for want of sugar – which the grocers indeed dislike selling for jam.

Aberdeen Journal, 8 August 1916

Mr Lawton claimed that salt could be used with the cheapest brown sugar, but May Byron's *Jam Book*, also published in 1916, warned against using 'cheap and inferior sugar, and beet sugar' as it 'spoils the colour and flavour' and 'deteriorates the keeping quality of the jam'. She suggested using:

liquid glucose (which is made from starchy materials such as maize) for sugar. Glucose should be added in the proportion of one and a quarter to one and a half parts of syrup for each one part of fruit … a cheap method, and glucose is said to be easier to digest than sugar; but most people prefer sugar.

Housewives were encouraged to find new ways of preserving fruit without using sugar:

SUGARLESS PLUM JAM

Put a gallon of elderberries into a preserving pan and cook them until the juice flows freely, then press and strain the juice through a sieve. Return to the pan and add two gallons of plums. Medium sized round plums should be used, just wiped with a cloth. When hot, add the grated rind of an orange and half a teaspoonful each of ground ginger and cinnamon. Simmer gently for two hours, skimming and stirring frequently. When cold, put into jars and cover in the usual way.

Southern Reporter, 13 September 1917

The Royal Horticultural Society wrote in the *Hull Daily Mail* on 22 June 1917: 'Not a plum or an apple, or any other fruit should be allowed to fall to the ground and rot.' The Food Production Department supplied home canners, cans, and bottles to individuals, and demonstrators showed how to use them. As many households still used an old-fashioned range, women could use the latent heat to dry fruit:

… put the largest purple plums into jars and dry them in a warm, closed oven for 2 or 3 hours, following this process up by spreading the plums on trays and drying them off with the door of the oven slightly ajar. The plums turned black but could be stored in bags or tins for a use when desired.

Aberdeen Journal, 2 October 1918

An article in *The Horticultural Advertiser* described a Canadian method developed by a Mrs Rudd, which would 'be of the greatest importance to the welfare of England':

Place the fresh fruit in any bottle that can be hermetically sealed by a rubber band; place the bottles in any receptacle that will hold 4 inches to 5 inches of water over the top of the bottles. Let the water tap run into each bottle with some force, to pack in fruit and wash out any impurities. Let the tap continue to run until the receptacle is full and running over. Then stop the tap. Wait about five minutes until all air bubbles have ceased to rise; then seal under the water. Take out bottles, wipe dry, and turn upside-down. If dry next morning you have a perfect job; if leaking, you must do again …

I need hardly point out to you the value of this process. It means the turning of the summer surplus into a valuable winter food at a minimum of cost and labour, and a great saving in sugar. It means that every family can help itself, and consequently help in solving the transportation problem.

Nelson Evening Mail, 3 November 1917

When the harvests of 1917 and 1918 were disappointing, housewives were encouraged to supplement their preserves with carrots, marrow and hedgerow fruits such as blackberries. The *Berwick Advertiser* suggested on 17 August 1917 that: 'Vegetable pulp can be mixed with fruit, such as marrow, swede, etc., and so every housewife can double her jam supply', whilst 'Economy' chose to use crabapples:

JAM AND THE FRUIT SCARCITY

To the Editor of the Birmingham Post.

Sir,—Having regard the scarcity and high price of fruit, may I suggest through your paper that marrow with crab[apple] … make a most delicious jam, being fruity in flavour, a lovely colour, and far nicer (to my taste) than plum jam. And as both marrows and crabs are plentiful this season, full advantage should be taken of the opportunity so offered to provide a large supply, at a moderate cost, of a really fine jam, free from stones and skins.

Prepare the marrow for cooking, cut in, say, one-inch squares, bake (without water) in a slow oven until well cooked, then strain as one would strain vegetables. To each pound of marrow pulp add one pint of crab juice – prepared exactly as for crab jelly – add 24oz of sugar (more or less), and cook as one would cook any other jam.

[from] Economy.

Birmingham *Daily Post*, 27 August 1918

As if all this was not enough, domestic jam-makers faced one further difficulty. The *Birmingham Mail* reported in September 1915: 'Jam jars are difficult to obtain from shops, though there should be no difficulty in collecting large numbers from the pantries and lumber rooms of private houses'. The shortage increased and in June 1918 the *Birmingham Mail* asked the public to 'mobilise your jam jars' to prevent fruit wastage. The distribution of jam jars to housewives in Pershore was undertaken by a new women's organisation, to whose history we shall now turn: the Women's Institute.

NOTES

1 R. Duffet, *The Stomach for Fighting: Food and the Soldiers of the Great War* (Manchester: MUP, 2012) p. 49.

2 M. Bramford, *Voices from the Past: Pershore 1900–1935* (Malvern: Aspect Design, 2015).

3 M. Byron, *May Byron's Jam Book* (London: Hodder and Stoughton, 1916).

6

NOT ALL JAM AND JERUSALEM: PERSHORE WOMEN'S INSTITUTE

The Pershore Women's Institute

Possibly the greatest legacy of the First World War for rural women was the introduction of the Women's Institutes (WI) in Britain.[1] From the outset the organisation attracted many women who had been involved in the struggles to enfranchise women, as Ray Strachey points out in *The Cause*, a history of the suffrage movement published in 1928:

> It is not too much to say that the lives of country women were transformed by the coming of this organisation, which brought instruction and variety just at the moment when enfranchisement and short skirts were bringing physical and mental development; and it is not surprising that women of all ages and classes who had worked in the suffrage movement turned their energies to this field.[2]

Pershore Women's Institute is now the oldest surviving WI in Worcestershire and, in 1916, was one of the very first branches to be formed in England.[3]

The Women's Institute Movement was originally founded in 1897 by Adelaide Hoodless in Stoney Creek in Canada, and swiftly aligned with the British Columbia Department of Agriculture who saw it as a means of organising women to improve rural food production and living conditions. Amongst the organisation's early executive officers was Mrs Madge Watt, of Collingwood, Ontario, a well-connected former professional journalist and campaigner for women's rights. In 1913, to avoid the scandal that surrounded her husband Alfred's suicide, Madge and her two sons sailed to England where she set about trying to persuade influential groups, including the government, that rural food production, preservation and preparation could be improved by the formation of Women's Institutes.

Although she made little headway in peacetime, the outbreak of war provided Mrs Watt with an advantage: national concerns over the food supply persuaded first the Agricultural Organisation Society and then the Board of Agriculture to employ her to promote Women's Institutes.

In 1915, Mrs Watt formed the very first British Women's Institutes in Wales and in Sussex, portraying the WI in her speeches as a means of enabling women to grow more food by working on the land and cultivating their gardens. She drew attention to the potential benefits of 'co-operative buying of seeds' and 'owning of garden tools', which would 'reduce the costs of small scale food production'. The WI motto 'For Home and Country' linked everyday domestic life to national interests and chimed well with the wartime ethos that the many tasks women undertook in their homes contributed to the war effort. Mrs Watt encouraged all members to ask: 'What is my home, my garden, my farm doing for my Country?'[5]

Mrs Madge Watt in wartime.
(By kind permission of Helen
Geissinger)

Pershore and Worcestershire more generally were inclined to the principles of co-operation, having already established co-operative marketing ventures. Hence on 1 March 1916 a public meeting to discuss the organisation of women to work on the land was held at the Shirehall in Worcester under the auspices of the County War Agricultural Committee. The meeting was chaired by Lord Coventry and attended by the great and the good of the county. Mrs Watt spoke in her role as the representative of the Agricultural Organisation Society. A further meeting was held on 30 October and reported in detail in both local and regional newspapers:

WOMEN ON THE LAND CONFERENCE AT WORCESTER

An important conference was held in Worcester, yesterday, of ladies and others interested in women's work on the land in Worcestershire. Viscountess Deerhurst presided, supported by Earl and Countess Coventry, the Countess of Plymouth, Viscount Cobham, Lady Hindlip, Lady Sandys, Lady Barbara Dudley Smith, Lady Isabel Margesson, Lady Georgina Vernon, Mr Stanley Baldwin, M.P., the Mayor of Worcester, and others.

Miss Day, Board of Agriculture organiser, described the co-operative system in operation at Upton-upon-Severn collecting garden produce from the small holders and cottagers. Speeches were also delivered on various aspects of agricultural work by Lady Hindlip, Mr G.F. Hooper, Lady Isabel Margesson, Miss Talbot, principal lady organiser of the Board of Agriculture, and representative farmers.

Birmingham Daily Post, 31 October 1916

By the time of this second big meeting, preparations were already underway to form WI branches in Pershore and Barnt Green. Mrs Watt's practice was to visit villages and towns and there explain the idea of a WI to the ordinary women of the area in order to drum up support to form an Institute and elect a committee, who would be responsible for its day-to-day running. In Worcestershire the stimulus to hold these first meetings often came from forceful and confident titled women, a prime example being Lady Isabel Margesson of Barnt Green. She and her daughter, Catherine, like a number of initial WI enthusiasts, had been suffragettes; indeed, Isabel chaired a meeting in Glasgow in September 1914 at which Mrs Pankhurst had been arrested amidst 'an outrage' which bordered on a riot. By 1916, Isabel and Catherine were busy organising women to work on the land or in local rural industries and to develop good parenting skills, and correctly saw the WI as aligned to these causes.

The Institutes were, as the name implies, for women, but the idea of starting WIs did not only appeal to women, some men were strong supporters too. A prominent fruit-grower in Pershore, and tireless president of the Co-operative

Market he helped to found, Geoffrey Fielder Hooper may have envisaged that instructing women in better domestic economy was a way of suppressing the local agricultural workers' and small-holders' need for higher wages. He wrote to the local newspaper to explain:

> If wives and daughters of small-holders and labourers with gardens could be shown how to utilize the products of their holdings in their daily diet in the way the French and Belgian women do, small-holders would have a far better chance of success and the value of 2s to 4s a week be added to their weekly earnings. Instruction and demonstration as to how this could be achieved would furnish a most fruitful work for the Ladies' Agricultural Organisation in rural districts.
>
> *Worcester Herald*, 4 November 1916

With the support of the Coventrys of Croome Park, Hooper and other wealthy market gardeners, Mrs Watt was invited to Pershore in the November of 1916 to set up a WI. The *Worcester Herald* reported the very first gathering of the Pershore Women's Institute:

> A meeting under the auspices of the Agricultural Organisation Society [A.O.S.] and Worcestershire War Agricultural Committee was held at the Masonic Hall on Tuesday night [21 November], where a discussion took place regarding the possibility of forming a Women's Institute in the town.
>
> The room was packed and much interest was shown in the proposed scheme. Viscountess Deerhurst (chairman of the War Agricultural Ladies' Sub-Committee) was announced to preside, but was unavoidably prevented from doing so. Mrs Geoffrey F. Hooper, who took her ladyship's place, spoke on the paramount need of increased food production, and paid a warm tribute to the good work which the Ladies' Committee were doing in training, helping and encouraging women to work on the land. 'We had got to use all possible man-power to thrash our enemies, and we should have to utilise all possible woman-power to take the place of the men in the fields of industry'. She quoted a letter from the Earl of Crawford, president of the Board of Agriculture, who said that 'we should have to depend entirely upon ourselves. We must make every use of lawful and honorable agencies at our command, and of these the help of women must be placed in the first rank. There was plenty of work on farms and in gardens, which women could do, and which in various parts of the country they were doing with the greatest success.'
>
> An address was given by Mrs [Madge] Watt from Canada, who has undertaken the initial organisation of Women's Institutes in this country, on behalf of the A.O.S. She congratulated Mrs Hooper on the splendid attendance, and said the interest and enthusiasm shown augured well for the success of the scheme

Pershore High Street in the early twentieth century, showing the Angel Inn and Posting House, at the back of which, in the Masonic Hall, the WI's first meeting was held. (Marshall Wilson Collection)

in Pershore. She said she understood [from] the result of the canvass amongst the women of Pershore [that] no less than 840 had volunteered to work on the land, and she had also learnt from the Chairman that no less than 400 men had gone from the town to serve the colours, which she considered a marvelous record. The speaker dealt in a very comprehensive manner with the aims and objectives of Women's Institutes, which she said were to study domestic economy, provide a centre for educational and social intercourse, encourage home and local industry, develop co-operative enterprises, and stimulate interest in the agricultural industry.

Worcester Herald, 25 November 1916

The members of Pershore WI

The women who attended the very first meeting of Pershore WI 100 years ago and became part of this innovative organisation were from a range of social backgrounds. Their ages varied, one or two were in their twenties or seventies, most were middle-aged. The majority were married, some had been widowed and others were single. Mrs Ferris's husband was a market gardener's labourer, whilst Mrs Gregory was married to a nightwatchman; Miss Roberts had retired from a life in domestic service and Mrs Russell was a charwoman. Predictably enough for a rural area in this era the role of Honorary President fell to a representative of the landed aristocracy: Virginia, Viscountess Deerhurst, who lived at Pirton Court and was wife to Lord Coventry's eldest son and heir.

An American by birth, Virginia married George, Viscount Deerhurst, in London in 1894. That she was independently wealthy would have been a relief to Viscount Deerhurst, an inveterate gambler, whose father had had to bail him out in 1901 by selling the valuable tapestries from Croome Court. Like her father-in-law the Earl, who was chair of the County Agricultural Committee, Virginia became actively involved in the organisation of rural workers during wartime, both as chair of the Women's Farm Labour Sub-Committee and, from 1918, of the Central Horticultural Sub-Committee, which sought to encourage food production by small growers and also arranged instruction in fruit and vegetable preservation such as canning and bottling.[6] Her adoption of the guiding principles of the WI movement as a means of increasing effective food production by organising rural people can be seen in the following letter:

FROM VISCOUNTESS DEERHURST TO MARKET GARDENERS AND FARMERS

Sir:— Now that there are possibilities of getting labour and infinite possibilities of marketing produce would it not be possible for every farmer and market gardener to grow at least a third more produce than they have been doing?

An increased food supply is of such vital importance to the nation, and Worcestershire is one of the few counties that are really looked to for help. Potatoes, parsnips, swedes, turnips, carrots, beetroot, celery, savoys, cabbage, onions etc., are all wanted for the Army now, and any grower or growers who can get together a truck load of vegetables, or two ton of roots, and put it on rail can sell direct to the Agricultural Produce Supplies, who are buying for the Army …

… where there are difficulties in getting sufficient produce together, my Committee will start collecting and packing centres, and will give all the advice and help they can, and when necessary will send a representative of the Agricultural Organisation Society to make the necessary arrangements.

VIRGINIA DEERHURST
Chairman Women's Farm Labour Sub-Committee, Shirehall, Worcester
Worcester Herald, 16 December 1916

The women who were elected as the first members of the Pershore WI committee to take on the day-to-day running of the Institute came from the more middling, professional classes in the town. They represented a number of key groups and included the wives of two doctors, a vet, the vicar and some of the wealthier fruit farmers. Many were already involved in civic and voluntary organisations in the town. The President, Mrs Rusher, lived with her doctor husband in a substantial house called The Paddocks on Worcester Street, while the role of Treasurer was allocated to the vet's wife, Mrs Jenny Rae Lees, who lived on Bridge Street. Committee member Mrs Phillips was the vicar's wife and had for many years been a nurse at the Cottage Hospital. As well as helping with her husband's ministry she was also heavily involved in running the Girls' Friendly Society. Mrs Edith Hooper, Branch Secretary, was married to Geoffrey Hooper, whose business and community connections were numerous, including membership of the Pershore Abbey Restoration Committee prior to the war. Edith was herself involved with a number of charities including the Soldiers, Sailors and Families Association (SSAFA), which looked after the welfare of wives and families of those in the services.

There were also women of more modest means on the committee such as Mrs Rosa Janet Edwards, wife of a post office clerk, and Miss Gertrude Annie Chick, a 39-year-old spinster who lived in Wisteria Cottage on Bridge Street and earned her living as a dressmaker. It is interesting to speculate whether Gertrude was pressured to take on the onerous role of Assistant Secretary and assiduous minute-taker, or whether perhaps she herself decided that involvement with the wives of many of the professional men of the town would provide her with useful contacts for her business.

For a number of these early members, the WI was a family affair. Schoolteacher Miss Edith Marie Brickell was a committee member and both her sisters were members. Similarly, a number of domestic servants attended: two from Mrs Hooper's household and two more from the household of the Beynons, who ran the Pomona Works. Again, one can only speculate about the motivations of those who attended the early WI in Pershore and whether their membership was a consequence of personal choice, gentle persuasion or social pressure. The majority of the members lived within walking distance of Pershore High Street, which provided the focus of their activities, but in time the committee took part in encouraging women in neighboring villages such as Eckington to start their own WIs.

What the WI did

Mrs Watt's speeches to local institutes indicate some fuzziness about exactly what the Institutes might do. In spring 1916, to one prospective group of women, she explained: 'Grants from the government enable lecturers and demonstrators to be sent from London and the meetings add social interests to the more solid advantages of addresses and talks on such varied subjects as domestic economy, small-holding and the use of artificial manures, cookery etc.'[7] Local Women's Institutes consequently developed in different ways in line with different local interests and circumstances.

In Pershore the WI used the Masonic Hall, behind the Angel Inn, as the venue for their monthly meetings, and paid 6s (£12 today) to have the use of the room, china, gas and a woman who made the tea and tidied up afterwards. The first meeting of the newly formed WI was held on 22 December and reported in the *Worcester Herald*:

THE WOMEN'S INSTITUTE

Viscountess Deerhurst, hon president, took the chair at the first meeting of the Women's Institute (affiliated to the A.O.S.) held at the Masonic Hall on Friday night. A demonstration of domestic cookery was given by Miss Richards, of the Worcestershire County Council and the hints she gave as to making soups will doubtless prove valuable. Miss Day, the official organiser of women's work, gave an address on 'Women on the Land' showing what great assistance might be rendered by women who were willing and properly organised. There was an exhibition of Red Cross appliances and comforts for the troops, and explanation given of the re-modeling of children's clothes. The social elements were provided by the older pupils of Miss Brickell's school.

Worcester Herald, 23 December 1916

The *Evesham Journal* noted that at this meeting:

The Hall was crowded, and the keenest interest was taken in the remarks of the lecturer, who gave numerous hints and illustrations, valuable alike to all her hearers no matter of what degree, station or income on 'How to make the most of our Food Rations.' A large gas stove (manipulated by Mrs G.F. Hooper, the hon secretary) turned out the complete article, which on being sampled by the judges was pronounced to be absolutely A1 – wonderfully economic for the pocket, nutritious for the body, and lastly in the order of things today, palatable to the taste.

Evesham Journal, 22 December 1916

The newspaper also pointed out that the Pershore Women's Institute was 'meeting with marked success, which its laudable objectives and excellent management deserves'.

As the nation's food shortages grew worse, food preparation became an increasing priority for the WI. In early 1917 the organisation wrote to the National Food Economy League to enquire as to the cost of lectures and courses; they also received short demonstrations in the use of maize, barley meal and oatmeal, in fruit bottling and the making of a really cheap nutritious soup. In the summer of 1917, the Pershore War Savings Association wrote to the WI to ask if they could start a War Communal Kitchen in the town, a proposal that was greeted with enthusiasm. The committee set about exploring the possibility of a grant and seeking further information on Travelling Kitchens from the Ministry of Food. The local newspapers reported:

COMMUNAL KITCHEN OPENS

A kitchen for the town was opened on Tuesday evening at the rear of the Pershore Club on premises which were readily adaptable and which are situated in a central position. The scheme was initiated by the Local War Savings Committee, and management afterwards taken over by the officials of the Women's Institutes … The Kitchen has been registered and the chief advantage of registration is the fact that if sugar and other commodities could not be obtained in sufficient quantities locally it will be supplied by the government. Mr G.F. Hooper advanced £10 towards initial expenses and for the opening day when over 130 meals were sold … The kitchen is open five days a week.

Worcester Herald, 21 July 1917

However, only one month later the minutes of the WI committee noted that there was 'agreement that the communal kitchen should be closed if it was not appreciated or paying its way'. Despite this setback the organisation went from strength to strength and by the end of the year it was reported that:

The newly formed Women's Institute shows no slackening of effort or enthusiasm, and the meeting held on Thursday evening last week was one of the best attended and most successful of any. The programme arranged by Mrs G.F. Hooper, of the Croft, combined both practical instruction and social enjoyment. An inspiring address on the New Year was given by the Vicar (the Rev. A.H. Phillips), Mr A. Ailsebrook speaking to a discussion on the subject of 'How Pershore can increase the food supply of the nation' advanced some valuable suggestions.

Mrs Harry Phillips, who for many years was matron of the Cottage Hospital, gave demonstrations in the art of first aid and bandaging, a body of youthful vocalists trained by Mrs J. Dolphin, of the Manse, afterward sang several carols in a praiseworthy manner: the ladies' choir contributed some stirring patriotic songs.

Evesham Journal, 17 December 1917

The drive to increase food production also led the WI to form pig and rabbit clubs, grow herbs, procure copies of potato recipes and arrange cookery demonstrations in Pershore and surrounding villages including Wyre, Wick and Defford in 1918. Miss Roberts, a retired domestic servant and WI member, served on the local Food Control Committee. As the name suggests, such committees were set up to stop profiteering and ensure food prices were controlled. They were often perceived as serving only the interests of the wealthy[8] but Miss Roberts' position would have ensured that working-class women also had a voice. The WI also worked with the Women's War Agricultural Committee to provide housewives in the district with jars for making jam, seed potatoes and seeds to grow vegetables.

Pershore WI encouraged women to take up a number of rural industries and crafts; organising demonstrations, instruction and competitions in basket-making, hat trimming, needlework and co-operative boot mending with instruction and tools and leather being procured for women to use. The money housewives saved mending the family footwear convinced many husbands that much was to be gained by their wives belonging to the WI. Their craft activities were also used to support men at the Front: women sewed and sent keepsakes and the WI obtained wool to knit garments and fabric to make shirts for men in the Worcestershire Regiment.

A handkerchief sent to soldiers at the Front. (Pershore Heritage Centre)

As an organisation for domestic women, Pershore WI, like the National Federation of Women's Institutes, took an active role in trying to improve the conditions of housewives' working lives. In May 1917, Miss Blyth inquired whether it would be possible for the WI to notify the local authority of the bad state of the drains and the need for a water supply in some areas of the town. At their October meeting in 1918, Mrs Edwards from Worcester spoke on the housing question:

> She emphasised the fact that women must spend their lives and do their work in a man-designed house making the best of a very bad article. The time had now come when women must think about what they really needed and how the interior of the house should be arranged.
>
> *Worcester Herald*, 19 October 1918

The WI in the inter-war period

For many housewives the support, advice and help of the Women's Institute was very welcome; little wonder that this organisation not only survived but thrived in the post-war era, providing a social hub and activities for women across the country and particularly in Pershore, when the WI opened its own hall in Priest Lane in October 1921.

The WI hall was a venue for classes in two inter-war crazes: folk dancing and keep fit; WI members also ran a library from here. The WI's commitment to charitable

Pershore WI at the opening of their new hall in 1921. (Pershore WI)

work and helping other women was a motivation for many of their activities. During the 1926 Miners' Strike, branch members sent parcels to mining areas; similarly, they organised annual Christmas parties for the inmates of the Pershore Poor Law Institution (or the workhouse, as it would commonly have been known).

Health care remained an important issue for the WI; members collected silver paper for the Worcester Maternity Fund, which provided a trained midwife to women in labour. Similarly, the 'Egg Roll Call', a popular element of many meetings, ensured Pershore Cottage Hospital received approximately 250 eggs a month, a welcome gift to a pre-NHS institution reliant on charitable donations. There were a number of doctors' wives and trained nurses on the first WI committee, so it is not surprising that the WI hall provided a welfare centre for young mothers, and many members assisted the district nurse in giving care and advice. In time a pram shelter was built behind the hall so that women did not have to lug a heavy pram up a flight of stairs when attending the clinics. When the Second World War broke out in 1939, Pershore WI expanded its activities to meet the new situation. The hall was used as a canteen for servicemen, serving over 1,000 cups of tea in one evening. Fruit preservation was again on the agenda – jam-making and also a canners club which utilized a canning machine kept in the WI hall.

NOTES

1 For a more detailed exploration of the early Women's Institute Movement, see M. Andrews, *The Acceptable Face of Feminism* (London: Lawrence and Wishart 1997, reprinted 2015).

2 R. Strachey, *The Cause* (London: Virago, 1928, reprinted 1969).

3 For a more detailed history of Women's Institutes in Worcestershire, 1918–1978, see Worcestershire Federation of Women's Institutes, *Madame President, fellow members: The Story of the Worcestershire Federation of Women's Institutes* (Worcester: The Federation, 1980).

4 Mrs Alfred Watt and N. Lloyd, *The First Women's Institute School* (London: NFWI Publication, 1918).

5 *Whitby Gazette,* 9 March, 1917.

6 WWAG Horticultural Sub-Committee and Women's Sub-Committee WAAS Accession no. 179. Reference no. 259.9:2. Parcel: 15.

7 *Reading Mercury,* 29 April 1916.

8 R. Van Emden and S. Humphries, *All Quiet on the Home Front* (London: Headline, 2003), pp. 215–16.

7

PERSHORE'S CHILDREN AT WAR

Emily Linney and University of Worcester
History Students

ლიე ჺჄ

The First World War affected the lives of even the smallest people in Pershore. Not only did children see their male relatives and neighbours don uniform and go off to fight, but they also observed the different roles and tasks their mothers and sisters took on. News of the conflict came into children's lives through the letters, deaths and injuries of relations. At school they learnt about the progress of the war at a personal, local and national level. In early November 1914, news of the Worcestershire Regiment's significant action during the Battle of Gheluvelt[1] spread across the county and entered the curriculum. In 1915, the County Education Committee issued a booklet to all schools entitled 'How the Worcestershires Saved the Day', which provided graphic descriptions of the battle; two years later, the Chairman offered prizes for the best essays on the battle. Victories could perhaps be romanticised but when on 18 April 1917 pupils at Hancock's Endowed School in Bredon learned that one of their former teachers had been killed in action, the shock of war came home.

Children were not merely passive or innocent victims of events. They actively engaged in and with the war effort in a number of ways: by joining youth organisations, working on the land and supporting charities. At school, lessons were interspersed with wartime activities: girls made socks, flannel shirts and blankets for refugees or soldiers on active service. During September 1914, the logbooks of St Mary's Church of England School in Hanley Castle recorded that such tasks delayed the girls' ordinary needlework classes, an indication of complaints to follow about the degree to which children's education was being sacrificed to the war effort. Such concerns were secondary to the need to feed the nation however; schoolchildren cultivated vegetables on school land and their harvests included potatoes, carrots, parsnips, turnips, beetroot, peas, lettuce and parsley. Most famously,

Worcestershire children ready with their baskets to go blackberry picking. (Berrow's Worcester Journal, *15 September 1918*)

in the latter years of the war, children engaged in the nationwide 'Great Blackberry Pick', collecting blackberries to make jam for 'soldiers and sailors'. The volume of blackberries collected and sent to jam factories was noted in school logbooks; for example, 1,171lbs of blackberries were collected by St Mary's during September and October 1918.

Clubs and uniforms

The most obvious and immediate involvement of children in the conflict was through established groups such as the Boy Scouts, Boys' Brigade, Cadet Force and Girl Guides[2] which at the time offered youngsters a chance to express their patriotism and, of course, to wear a uniform. Some parents, with money to spare, also had miniature soldier outfits made up for their sons, and nursing costumes for their daughters, enabling them to identify with the war effort.

The immediate need, at the outbreak of war, was to harvest the fruit ripening on the trees and Boy Scouts were quickly identified for this role:

A CALL ON BOY SCOUTS

Following this meeting, a joint meeting of the National Farmers' Union and the Market Gardeners was held. The effect of the commandeering of horses and the recalling of men to the colours was considered. It was generally agreed that [...] the selection and commandeering had been carried out by those in authority with as much care as possible in order to avoid inconvenience.

Discussion followed as to the possibility of a lack of carters for carrying the harvest. It was thought this would be met by the labourers already available, but in the event of a shortage it was decided to ask the local officials of the Boy Scouts to help in this ... It is hoped that labour will be plentiful in helping, because the crops are abundant.

Worcester Herald, 15 August 1914

The following year, Boy Scouts and Manchester Grammar School pupils gave up their summer holidays to pick fruit:

The Boy Scouts, of whom there are a large number in the district, are devoting their energies to helping the market gardeners pick fruit, and they are proving themselves a valuable asset to growers in the present shortage of skilled labour.

Worcester Herald, 31 July 1915

The importance of the Scouts' work in the district was acknowledged by the movement's founder, Robert Baden-Powell, who visited Pershore with his wife, Olave, to inspect the boys and receive a basket of plums:

VOLUNTEERS AND SCOUTS AT PERSHORE: ADDRESS BY GENERAL BADEN-POWELL

A church parade took place at the Abbey Church, Pershore, on Sunday morning, members of the Volunteer Training Corps and various patrols of Boy Scouts attending. The procession, which was headed by a military band from Norton Barracks, was about 700 strong ... The Pershore and District Boy Scouts and Boys' Brigade were joined by the 1st and 2nd Malvern Platoons, the Coldwell, Upton-upon-Severn, Hampton contingents, and the 12th Birmingham Brigade. Most of the lads who are visitors are camping out in various parts of the Pershore district, rendering valuable aid in fruit-picking to growers.

The Chief Scout, General Sir Robert Baden-Powell, accompanied by Lady Powell, attended Divine service, and afterwards inspected the lads, who were drawn up at the Co-operative Fruit Market. Sir Robert paid compliment to the boys on their smart appearance, and emphasised the importance of the patrol leaders sticking fast to their duties, for it was not unlikely that it would fall to their lot to keep the brigades together, should the scoutmasters be wanted for other work. The Government recognised the boys of England were doing good work, and greater responsibilities would probably be given them in the future.

Before dismissing, cheers were given the General and a lad from the local platoon presented her ladyship with a basket of Pershore plums ...

Birmingham Daily Post, 3 August 1915

General Sir Robert and Lady Olave Baden-Powell receive a basket of Pershore plums. (Berrow's Worcester Journal, *9 August 1915)*

Agriculture was only one of a range of activities with which the Scouts engaged: they also delivered messages, collected scrap, and were 'patients' for Red Cross trainees keen to practice their bandaging. Belonging to the Scouts gave many boys a sense that they were part of the war, even their uniform could be seen to align them with those in military dress. For those boys keen to carry out activities which more directly prepared them to join the forces, Pershore swiftly acquired both a Boys' Brigade and a Cadet Corps:

BOYS' BRIGADE FORMED

A well-attended meeting, held at the Masonic Hall, Pershore, on Wednesday, resulted in the inauguration of a local branch of the Boys' Brigade movement. The chair was taken by Mr H.J. Hadley, Captain of the Worcester Company, who was supported by Lieut. W. Day, Mr G. Foss, and Mr H.J. Millard. A lantern lecture illustrating in detail the work of the Boys' Brigade, occupied the greater portion of the time of the meeting.

The chairman and the organisers emphasised that the Boys' Brigade was not to be regarded as in opposition to the Boy Scouts in Pershore, the speakers declaring that they had the highest regard for that movement, and would like to work and co-operate with the troop. But it was thought – and the large attendance of boys at the meeting justified the position – that something should be done for those who were not members of the Scouts. If a company of the brigade was formed, it had been decided that no boy should be allowed to join if he belonged to the Scouts, unless, in fact, he had ceased to be a member of that body at least three months, or for other substantial reasons.

Captain Hadley gave an interesting account of the growth of the Brigade, and spoke of the work of the Worcester Brigade, which had been in existence for more than 12 years. Several of the early members were now serving their King and Country at the Front. At the close about 40 lads, whose ages ranged from 12 to 18 years gave in their names to form a branch, and seven or eight young men were elected officers. Mr Millard was elected Captain *pro tem* and Mr Robert Dowty accepted the office of Secretary.

Worcester Herald, 3 October 1914

The Boys' Brigade was not just about learning drill. Lads from Birmingham units spent their summer in Pershore, their patriotic fervour directed into helping with the fruit harvest:

BOYS' BRIGADE RETURN FROM FRUIT PICKING

The 12th Birmingham (St Cuthbert's) Company of the Boys' Brigade recently returned from Pershore, after three weeks of fruit picking. Forty boys […] and five officers went on the trip, and camped on the Croft Farm, kindly lent by Mr G. Hooper. Owing to the rain which fell in the first few days it was necessary to […] billet the boys in the Parish Gymnasium, where they remained.

The boys worked in the orchards from 6.50 a.m. to 5.30 p.m., each boy earning 12s per week, besides extra pocket money at the rate of ½d per pot of fruit picked

Pershore Boys' Brigade enjoy a tea party. (Berrow's Worcester Journal, *15 June 1915*)

(some of the boys picking six to seven pots per day) … The Pershore people were very kind to the boys, and on their arrival at New Street Station they looked well cared for and full in health, happiness, and plums …

The camp was arranged from a patriotic motive as the shortage of labour in harvesting the fruit is no doubt a serious matter, and it seemed that each boy realised this and tried to fulfil his company's motto, *Non mihi, sed patriae* [not for myself, but my country].

Birmingham Mail, 28 August 1915

For lads who really wanted to start training for the army, the newly formed Cadet Corps was a must:

CADET CORPS

In response to the urgent recommendation of the Worcestershire Territorial Association, a Cadet Corps has been formed in connection with the Pershore Company of the Worcestershire Volunteer Regiment. Drills are now being conducted by Volunteer N.C.Os, under Lieut. H. Clifford, in the Drill Hall, Pershore, at 8 p.m. on Tuesdays and Fridays, when recruits can be enrolled. The age limit fixed by the Territorial Association is 12 and 17, but it is hoped to obtain a large number of the older boys.

There should be sufficient material in Pershore to form a strong Corps without interfering with existing organisations. The advantages of drill and discipline […] are manifest, apart from the spirit of patriotism, which boys should be glad to display. If there is sufficient support for the movement, and a prospect of interest being permanent, it is proposed to start a clubroom in connection with the Corps. It is also intended to form a String Band, under an efficient instructor.

Worcester Herald, 1 September 1915

Many years afterward, Cyril Smith reminisced about his days in the Cadet Corps:

In 1916, I joined the Cadets. They were led by Captain Clifford, who lived at Endon Hall, by Wick. We had a lovely band and we used to have route marches to all the churches – Drakes Broughton, Defford, Elmley Castle and others. Lovely nights we had at the drill hall in Defford Road, drill, shouting and everything to keep us fit. They were getting us ready to be called up for war, but the war was over by 1918. They still ran Cadets after the war, and I think they are still going now.

Cyril Smith's Memoirs (Pershore Heritage Centre Collection)

Agnes Baden-Powell visits Worcestershire in 1918. (Courtesy of Girlguiding Worcestershire)

The girls of the town had to wait until September 1918 for Miss Joan Elkington to form the 1st Pershore Guide Company. The Guides paraded for the first time at the Armistice Service at the abbey on 17 November 1918, watched by Miss Agnes Baden-Powell, Chief Guide.

Work

Worcestershire had a long tradition of employing children on the land and this practice increased significantly during the conflict. Local Attendance Officers revealed that as the war progressed, children's school attendance in the county dropped, as reported in the *Worcester Herald* on 16 June 1917:

School attendance figures in Worcestershire
1914	91.1%
1915	90.1%
1916	89.1%
1917	85.4%

These figures include children absent from school due to illnesses such as colds, influenza, whooping cough, impetigo, or because of heavy rain or snow. However, significant absences were caused by the need for boys and girls to work on the land to produce food for the war effort, particularly in Pershore and the Vale where labour-intensive smallholdings created one of the highest employment rates for child labour in the county.

The Coombs family at harvest time. (Marshall Wilson Collection)

Children help to raise funds for the POWs at Pershore Farmers Sale. (Berrow's Worcester Journal, 1918)

Children helped with haymaking and the harvest, gathering produce including plums, blackberries, hops and peas. This sort of seasonal work had a strong historical precedent in the area: in 1872 Mr Varden, owner of a 250-acre market garden, explained during a discussion on the Agricultural Children's Employment Bill that at harvest he had a demand for '200 or 300 women and children,' adding, 'I do not employ the children but pay the mothers for the quantity of fruit picked. Schools in the surrounding districts are closed for the time ... The babies are placed under the hedge in the charge of older children'.[3] Such practices continued during wartime. Mr Deakin, who had contracts with the army to supply strawberries, engaged nearly 300 women in fruit picking. Such work often required so many children to be absent from lessons that schools were compelled to close for the harvest from July to September.

Until 1918 the school leaving age was 12, although parents or farmers frequently applied to the County Education Committee for a 'Certificate of Exemption' which permitted children below this age to engage in full or part-time work. For example, on 2 July 1915, Earls Croome Church of England Primary School removed four boys from the register who had been granted certificates by the Upton Education Committee. The following year, a farmer put in an application for an 11-year-old boy to work on his land. Understandably, some teachers had concerns:

CHILD LABOUR ON FARMS
TEACHERS CRITICISE WORCESTERSHIRE COUNTY COUNCIL

Mr W. Scott Carrack, Oldbury, presided at the annual meeting of the Worcestershire Teachers' Association at Worcester on Saturday ... Mr T. Thompson, of Redditch, gave an address on the depletion of rural schools and suggestions teachers could make towards a solution of the problem. He thanked two members of the association – Mr Taylor and Mr Church – for their opposition to the resolution passed on the subject of child labour by the Worcestershire County Council.

The County Council's resolution whereby any child of eleven should attend school four half-days and work six almost took one's breath away. He suggested, as an alternative to what was proposed, that school hours should be from 8.30 till 11, and from 12 to 2, setting children free after the latter hour.

It was decided to send a resolution to the County Education Committee protesting against the reactionary policy of allowing boys of eleven to work on farms, and asking them to reconsider their decision. Mr Stiles (Malvern) said the decision of the committee was a disgrace to our civilisation. The committee was composed of land magnates, who were capitalists, whose benefit it was to get labour as cheaply as possible.

Mr Frank Roscoe, secretary of the Teacher's Registration Council, also referred to the County Council's decision on child labour and said that action did not indicate a genuine belief in the value of education. (Applause.)

Evesham Journal, 4 March 1916

Some children undertook work on a more casual basis, only telling the school the reason for their absence after they had completed the job. Logbooks record how others, attempting to balance work with attendance, laboured on the land outside school hours and had to be sent home for falling asleep during morning lessons. Newspaper articles described absences as 'a very serious matter' and included details of cases of parents being fined up to £1 2s 6d (nearly £50 today) for failing to send their children to school. Parents' explanations included the necessity for older children to stay at home to care for younger siblings while their mothers were at work:

SCHOOL ATTENDANCE CASE

Henry Pitt (40), of Defford Common, was summoned by Mr Cyril Francis White, School Attendance Officer, Eckington, for not sending his children, Alice and Annie, to school. Mr White proved the case. Mrs Pitt said she kept the children away to mind the other children while she went to work on the land and besides this, the school was three miles away. Fined 6d in each case.

Worcester Herald, 21 August 1915

In another case, children turned up neither to school nor work:

SCHOOL ATTENDANCE CASES

Charles Burr (50), labourer, The Newlands, Pershore, was summoned by Mr C.F. Stratton, School Attendance Officer, Pershore, for not sending his child, Ethel, to school. Mr Stratton said the child had only attended 27 times out of a possible 47 during the past six weeks. She was 10 years of age. There were two previous convictions. Fined 10s.

Ernest Payne (40), labourer, Bredon's Hardwick, was summoned by Mr C.F. White, School Attendance Officer, Eckington, for not sending his child, Ernest, to school. Defendant did not appear, but sent an apology to the Court, pleading guilty, and saying that the reason he did not send the lad to school was that they had run short of bread, and sent him out for some.

Mr Stratton said the Education Committee brought the case forward because it was a common practice at Bredon's Hardwick to keep the children away from school for a considerable time after they had become of school age. Fined 10s.

Worcester Herald, 23 June 1917

With the scope to leave school at 12, boys could work for a number of years before they could join the forces. This made them appealing employees and lads sometimes took on what in a pre-war era would have been considered men's work in agriculture and in factories. The long hours of work could be dangerous:

ACCIDENT

Harry Young, a lad of 14, the 6th son of Mr and Mrs G. Young, of Knight's Building, Pershore, had his hand badly mutilated on Tuesday, in a printing machine […] where he was employed, and was taken to the Cottage Hospital and detained. Some two or three years ago he was impaled on a fence, and the thumb of his left hand was so injured it had to be amputated. It is most probable that the accident he sustained on Tuesday will necessitate the removing of the thumb, and perhaps the first finger also, of the right hand.

Worcester Herald, 28 July 1917

The wages children received rarely reflected the danger or the arduous nature of their work or their skills, particularly if they worked on the land, and this caused some controversy:

CHILDREN ON THE LAND – A CASE OF LOW WAGES

The Elementary Education Sub-Committee reported, with reference to the employment of school children, that the number of attendances lost through children being absent in employment on the land for the year ended February 28 was 216,328, representing a reduction in the grant of £1,050. The attendances lost in each district were: … Droitwich 1,426, Evesham 22,780 … Malvern 3,092 … Pershore 52,307 … Upton-upon-Severn 17,934.

The Chairman referred to the disparity in the figures for the different districts … In certain districts people seemed to consider that two boys were equal to a man, and consequently they stated that they had two boys from school …

Mr C. Wright quoted the case of a boy between 12 and 13 who was employed from 7 in the morning till 6 at night, and from 8 in the morning till 12 noon on Sundays. He had all his meals at home, and for the first six weeks he received 4s. a week, and for the second five weeks 5s. a week. The payment worked out at seven-eighths of a penny per hour …

He thought that a certain amount of child labour was needed in the country to-day, but when he told them that the firm with which he was associated would have given such a boy 9s. a week, they would see that child labour was being exploited for the benefit of some farmers, and the country was suffering accordingly …

In some cases it was almost child slavery, and he was sure that it was never the view of the County Council that child labour should be exploited in this disgraceful manner.

Evesham Journal, 19 May 1917

Beyond work and uniforms

Children's support for the war effort extended to fund-raising for charities. Serbian and Belgian refugees, soldiers blinded or wounded in action, and the Jack Cornwell VC Memorial Fund all benefitted from Pershore schools' fund-raising activities and in November 1918, Bishampton School raised £100 for the War Savings Association.

Patriotic distractions such as egg collections for wounded soldiers and performances in pageants and fêtes kept children occupied:

SUNDAY SCHOOL FÊTE

A fête in connection with the Sunday School was held in the Abbey Grounds on Thursday afternoon. The proceedings opened with a procession around the town, with the Choir, Sunday School members, decorated cars, and band. Afterwards there was a festival service at the Abbey, a sermon being preached by the Rev. A.A. Cockle (Vicar of Stoulton). The children then went to the Abbey grounds, where, in spite of heavy rain, they had tea.

[Despite] the rain continuing … it was eventually agreed to carry out the programme, and the sports were held.

The events included tug-of-war, a cycle gymkhana, sideshows, and various other attractions. The proceeds will be devoted to the Red Cross Society and the Sunday School Fund. The Rev. Allen, of Pershore, was responsible for the arrangements, and to him praise is due. He was assisted by many ladies and gentlemen (including Miss Handy, the School Superintendent), and all worked hard under dispiriting circumstances. The decorated cars were much admired.

The tableau illustrated the 'Catholic Church's appeal to the Allies.' There was one regrettable mishap, a boy falling off the cars. He was picked up unconscious. He was sent home and soon recovered. Dancing took place in the evening …

Worcester Herald, 7 August 1915

Even in wartime children were children, and not always as committed to the war effort as might be imagined. Two 14-year-old lads were brought before the magistrates for causing malicious damage to cherry trees in Fladbury by throwing stones and deliberately breaking off branches. The *Worcester Herald* report of 7 July 1917 suggests that the two boys were those unfortunate enough to be caught

Children in the Peace Parade, outside Brown's Shop in the High Street. (Marshall Wilson Collection)

and that many village children had enjoyed the game. The guilty pair were only prevented from receiving a birching by their fathers' intervention and each boy was fined.

When peace was finally declared in July 1919, it was apt that the children celebrated first:

> On Saturday afternoon the children, between 500 and 600 in number, paraded the town, headed by the Cadet Corps Band and had tea in the Abbey Grounds. Sports were held on the following Monday
>
> *Worcester Herald*, 19 July 1919

NOTES

1 The main reference work for the Worcestershire Regiment in the war is the history written as part of the County War memorial, by Captain H. Stacke, *The Worcestershire Regiment in the Great War* (Kidderminster: Cheshire & Sons, 1928).

2 For further exploration of youth organisations see John Springhall, *Youth, Empire and Society* (London: Croom Helm, 1977).

3 R.C. Gaut, *A History of Worcestershire Agriculture and Rural Evolution* (Worcester: Littlebury Press, 1939).

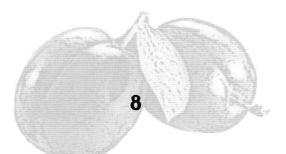

8

LIFE GOES ON in PERSHORE

*Pershore Heritage and History Society and
University of Worcester History Students*

⟨⟨⟨ ⟩⟩⟩

War disrupted, displaced and even destroyed some of the families and communities in Pershore and yet in spite of the hostilities day-to-day life continued to combine the mundane and the extraordinary, romance and marriage, birth and death. Seemingly frivolous leisure activities could be turned into patriotic events, imbued with nationalistic dialogue and charitable endeavour. Residents encountered new inconveniences during evening outings when the blackout was introduced due to fears of Zeppelin raids and bombing. Street lighting was reduced in 1916 and Inspector Pegg, of Pershore Police Division, announced that should hostile aircraft or Zeppelins enter British airspace, the tenor bell of St Andrew's church would be rung as a warning to the populace.

The following August, the landlord of the Three Tuns Hotel was summoned before the magistrates for failing to shade the lights in his drawing room on

The Three Tuns Hotel in Broad Street, Pershore. (Marshall Wilson Collection)

19 August. Police Sergeant Drew reported that at 10.30 p.m. he noticed a bright light coming from the hotel window; the blind was not drawn at all and bright lights reflected across Broad Street. For flouting the blackout regulations, the landlord was fined 10*s* (about £25 today).

Pubs and pastimes

The public house occupied a significant role in working-class culture during the Edwardian period that was undiminished in wartime. Concern over selling strong drink to servicemen produced a flurry of prosecutions, including one for selling uniformed troops alcohol, which they subsequently drank at the roadside in Lower Moor, south of Pershore, in September 1914.

The *Worcester Herald* reported the case of John Wood (59) and Elizabeth Wood (42), both labourers of no fixed abode, who were found drunk and disorderly in Charlton. Apparently they had:

> been creating a disturbance, using very bad language and the woman was especially violent and used filthy language and tried to bite the policeman's hand. They were only taken into custody with some difficulty.
>
> *Worcester Herald*, 10 July 1915

Concern about the impact of alcohol consumption on wartime industrial and agricultural production led the government to introduce regulations under the Defence of the Realm Act (known as DORA). This restricted pub opening hours for the first time, reduced the strength of beer and made it illegal either to treat a friend to a drink or buy alcohol on credit by running up a slate. This did not abate concern about the influence of alcohol on workers who had the opportunity to

Will Haynes at the Star public house in Bridge Street, Pershore. (Nancy Fletcher)

earn higher wages in wartime than they had before. Enthusiasts for the Temperance movement encouraged people to take the 'Pledge' and give up alcohol by linking the virtues of abstinence to the fulfillment of patriotic duty, as a report on a meeting of the Pershore Temperance Society in 1915 made clear:

> The Rev. J. Willis spoke on temperance and its benefits to the individual and the country. Miss Hawley gave a rousing patriotic speech. Tea was served in a large marquee. After tea Miss Hawley addressed the gathering and announced 30 pledges had been taken at the tea tables. They must bear in mind all that the soldiers had done and were doing (especially the Worcesters). They were all proud of all the praise, which the whole world had for them. She hoped all the women would try to provide good homes for them all when they return.
>
> *Worcester Herald*, 10 July 1915

The Teetotallers' campaign continued throughout the war; in August 1917, the Women's Temperance Society opened a coffee stall in the Co-operative Market and the Revd J. Willis, the vicar of Defford, argued that: 'abstaining from alcohol over a long spell had been amply proved to improve a man's output at work', and thus aid the war effort. Despite their exhortations, alcohol remained something of an issue during the conflict.

Joseph Welsh, a 63-year-old rag-and-bone collector, was charged with being drunk and disorderly when he assaulted a policeman with a poker, used obscene language and broke windows in his own house. Reporting the case on 7 August 1915, the *Worcester Herald* recorded that PC Clegg said: 'the defendant was harmless when sober but like a mad man when drunk' and that 'it was a very serious offence to strike an officer with a poker'. A couple of weeks later, on 21 August 1915, the *Worcester Herald* reported that PC Clegg's colleague, PC Mann, gave evidence at the Petty Sessions about a soldier who became excessively drunk when: 'he had met some pals and had a little jollification and more beer than was good for him.' In his inebriated state the soldier had not only used filthy language but also kicked and attempted to bite the policeman. He was found guilty and fined 2*s* 6*d* for being drunk and 10*s* for assaulting a policeman, a stiff penalty when an infantry private earned approximately 1*s* 6*d* per day before deductions.

A report from the Pershore Licensing Sessions, published in early 1916, suggests that, despite there being one licensed house to every 194 residents in the division, the incidence of drunkenness amongst locals had not greatly increased. Only 'twenty-three persons had been proceeded against for drunkenness and twenty-two convicted. Of those convicted eighteen were non-residents. There was an increase of one person convicted compared with the previous year.' However, the newspaper reported that the Revd Willis had not given up his fight against the demon drink:

TOO MANY INNS AT DEFFORD

The Rev. J. Willis, vicar of Defford, drew the attention of the Bench to the fact that there were seven licensed houses to a population of 450. He asked if the Bench could see their way to reduce the number. The Bench said they had considered the matter but there was no prospect of their being able to do anything at present.

Gloucestershire Echo, 2 February 1916

Even in wartime, or perhaps because of it, both locals and people from further afield needed relaxation; consequently many traditional activities continued throughout the duration. Pershore, with its fair climate and scenic views, was a popular destination for day-trips by river, road and rail. Newspapers carried reports of visits from Sunday schools, church choirs, the Conservative clubs of Cheltenham, the Bristol Corn Trade Clerks' Guild and, in summer 1915:

> ... about 350 soldiers – Belgian and British – billeted in the various Red Cross Hospitals in [Cheltenham], had an afternoon's outing in motor-cars, proceeding as far as Pershore where they were entertained to tea by Mr W. Unwin. 'The Day' must be voted a great success.
>
> *Western Daily Press*, 4 June 1915

In autumn 1916, the *Worcester Herald* reported that Pershore had had an influx of visitors on Bank Holiday Monday: 'business premises kept open as usual. The weather was enticing to lovers of outdoor recreation. The river claimed many patrons for boating, while many went fishing, which sport is now getting fairly good.' The river provided an extra draw as angling competitions continued throughout the war. The *Evening Despatch* 'Rod & Line' column reported on 31 May 1918: 'despite the difficulties of travelling many Birmingham clubs are making arrangements to hold their annual contests, the venues selected including Evesham, Defford, Wyre (for Pershore), and Holt Fleet'. Even these seemingly safe and innocuous pastimes provided the potential for tragedy and there were numerous newspaper reports of people, particularly youngsters, drowning in the river when swimming or fishing.

Cycling and other peacetime leisure occupations carried on into war, but the local hockey club cancelled its fixtures for the duration. The Croome Hunt met on a regular basis throughout the war, somehow managing to employ men as hunt servants and retain a number of horses, which might otherwise have been used for the war effort. The annual horse fair also continued, but horse racing did not: it had been frequent before the war, but there was criticism when Pershore races were held in 1915, and further meets were cancelled. For entertainment, Pershore people attended concerts at the Music Hall, pageants, plays or social events at other

Doris and Fanny Cole in Station Road, Pershore. (Cynthia Johnson)

meeting places in town, many of which served to raise both spirits and funds for war charities. The Cottage Hospital was a regular recipient of charity; in February 1916 donations went to provide comforts for the 1st Worcestershire Regiment at the Front while in 1917 'an enjoyable whist drive' was held in aid of the Young Men's Christian Association Club, occupied at that date by soldiers drafted into town for musketry practice.

Charities

During four years of war a cacophony of voices arose championing the 18,000 charities established at local and national level to provide medical care or support for servicemen and their families. This was a time when there was no welfare state and limited provision for the wives and dependents of men who were incapacitated or killed in conflict. Charitable causes required volunteers to devise innovative activities and compete to raise funds.

In Pershore, charitable activity began immediately after war broke out with parish collections for the Prince of Wales Relief Fund, which helped look after the wives and children of servicemen. A concert was held at the Ship Inn to raise funds in September 1914 and a local committee was set up for the Soldiers, Sailors and Families Association. Local farmers and the Co-operative Market organised fund-raising activities. Following the harvest in 1914, Pershore Fruit Growers' Association sent a splendid consignment of apples to the sailors on duty in the North Sea and sold and resold a 'plump little pumpkin' to raise £2 5s 3d (about £100 today) although its intrinsic value was only 3d (60p). The fruit growers continued to send their produce to the forces, sending 2,720lbs of Pershore plums in August 1916 alone. Pumpkins weren't the only gourds to raise money – a marrow from Badsey played an important role:

THE TALE OF THE MARROW

A greengrocer who carries on business in Villa Road, Handsworth, recently purchased a pot of vegetables from the Wholesale Market, Smithfield, and on taking them out for sale, she discovered scratched upon one: '*It is the wish of Mr —— of Badsey, Worcestershire, that the purchaser of this marrow should sell it for the Red Cross Fund.*'

The words, which had been scratched on when the marrow was very small, could be read quite distinctly. The marrow was not full grown and had evidently been cut inadvertently. The purchaser, however, determined that it should not go into the pot before its mission had been accomplished.

She exhibited it to her customers, and had the satisfaction of collecting £2.5s.6d, which she handed over, together with the marrow, to the Red Cross Fund.

The Birmingham Daily Mail, 23 September 1916

Some of the more innovative fund-raising activities such as guessing the weight of the pig, fancy fairs, whist drives, bazaars and dances allowed those on the home front to have fun without feeling unpatriotic. So the potentially frivolous Garden Fête held in the Abbey Grounds during the 1917 August Bank Holiday, fulfilled the serious purpose of raising funds for Pershore Cottage Hospital and Universities Mission to South Africa. Likewise, the proceeds of Pershore Social Club activities were sent to the Worcestershire Prisoners of War Comfort Fund to benefit British soldiers held captive abroad. 1917 was a good year for POW charities: Pershore Board of Guardians and District Council sent £100 in four instalments to the Prisoners of War Fund whilst the Worcestershire County Association for Prisoners of War sought to raise £12,000 a year (equivalent to a phenomenal £516,000 today), which was sent to troops in Germany and Turkey.

Jumble sales were particularly popular as they not only raised funds and provided a social diversion, but they also enabled locals, particularly the less well-off, to conform to the wartime ethos of avoiding waste and buy clothes and other household necessities at a reasonable price. However, it's clear that some jumble sales erred rather more towards being frivolous society occasions than others. Indeed, as the following report indicates, some gained the patronage of local elite:

PATRIOTIC JUMBLE SALE A PERSHORE EFFORT

The Pershore farmers, fruit growers and townspeople united in arranging a jumble sale for patriotic funds on Tuesday …

There was a wide response to the appeal for contributions and these made an imposing array at the Co-operative Market. The entries of livestock included sheep, pigs, a calf, fowls etc. and the miscellaneous entry of produce included a large supply of seed and eating potatoes. In fact one was surprised to see so many potatoes remaining. One lady sent half a ton of seed …

The first lot was quite out of the ordinary even for these days of uncommon lots for charity. It was none other than the 'Mayor' of Pershore, Mr P. Hanson or 'Sir Peter' as the catalogue announced him. The bidding for the 'Mayor' was on the understanding that the last purchaser should retain not Mr Hanson but a very 'vivid' portrait of him painted 'by one who ought to be shot'. The large audience present entered into the spirit of the sale and this 'lot' was an excellent send off to more serious business … and eventually Mr F.R. Pearson became the purchaser at £3.

A number of ladies worked enthusiastically in selling tickets for competitions amongst which was one for guessing Lord Coventry's correct weight. Quite early in the afternoon these guesses varied from 9 to 14 stone.

Worcester Herald, 25 April, 1917

A wartime romance

Romance and courtship was not restrained by wartime, indeed the uncertainty of the first days of the war gave a sudden impetus to couples to marry whilst they could. The *Worcester Herald* reported that on 12 August 1914, Arthur Mayo, a 29-year-old postman who lived in Bridge Street, Pershore, married Frances Edith Ellis, also 29 and a schoolteacher originally from Gloucester.

The story of Fanny and Tom illustrates very clearly how despite, or even because of the turbulent times, many couples met, courted, married and made a new life in the post-war world. Some were couples who might never have met in peacetime because of where they lived or who they were. Fanny Cole was a

*A wedding in Pershore. (*Berrow's Worcestershire Journal, *1 December 1917)*

A local wedding. (Cynthia Johnson)

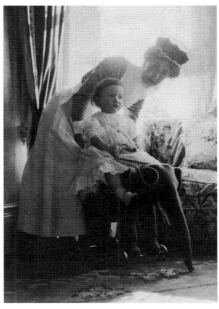

Fanny Cole, children's nursemaid. (Cynthia Johnson)

Thomas Slaney (on the left) in his uniform. (Cynthia Johnson)

country girl born in Pinvin in 1893, who had taken a number of positions as a children's nurse at various big houses near Pershore before going to work in Birmingham. Tom Slaney was a city boy born in Birmingham in 1890, who became a soldier in 1912.

At the onset of war, Tom was posted abroad but in November 1914 was shot and possibly gassed, which resulted in him temporarily losing the use of his legs. He was treated at the VAD unit in Olton, Solihull, before being sent to convalesce at Highbury Hall, Birmingham. It was during this convsalescence that he spied a young children's nurse taking her charges out for fresh air near Highbury Hall, was smitten and courted her for two years.

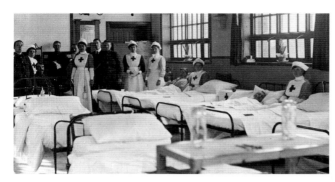

Tom in bed at the VAD Unit, Olton. (Cynthia Johnson)

Tom convalescing at Highbury Hall. (Cynthia Johnson)

A postcard of The Avenue, Workman Gardens, Evesham, where Tom and Fanny spent a happy day together. (Cynthia Johnson)

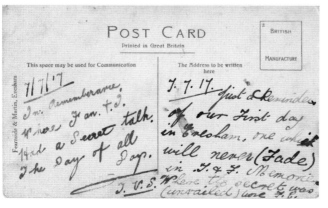

Tom's message on the back of the postcard. (Cynthia Johnson)

Fanny and Tom's courtship, like many wartime relationships, was largely carried out at a distance through the exchange of letters, poetry and postcards and affirmed by small keepsakes.

SOMEBODY'S DARLING

Into the ward of the white washed halls
Where the wounded and dying lay
Wounded by bayonets, shots and shells
Somebody's Darling was borne one day
Somebody's Darling so young and so brave
Wearing yet on his pale sweet face
Soon to be hid in the dust of the grave
The lingering light of the boyhood face.

Matted and damp are the curls of gold
Kissing the snow of that fair young brow
Pale are the lips of delicate mould –
Somebody's Darling is dying now
Back from the beautiful blue-veined brow
Brush all the wandering waves of gold
Cross his hands on his bosom now
Somebody's Darling is still and cold.

Kiss him once for somebody's sake
Murmur a prayer soft and low
One bright curl from its fair mates take
They were somebody's pride you know
Somebody's hand had rested there
Was it a mother's soft and white
And have the lips of a sister fair
Been baptized in the waves of light.

God knows best, he was somebody's love
Somebody's heart enshrined him there
Somebody wafted his name above
Night and morn on the wings of prayer
Somebody wept when he marched away
Looking so handsome, brave and grand
Somebody's kiss on his forehead lay
Somebody clung to his parting hand.

Somebody's waiting and watching for him
Yearning to hold him again to her heart
And there he lies with his blue eyes dim
And the smiling childlike lips apart.

By Fanny Cole (1893–1981). Written in 1914
Reproduced by kind permission of Cynthia Johnson

After just over two years of courtship, letters and brief outings, Tom married Fanny on 1 April 1918 in St Nicholas church, Pinvin. Brought together by the circumstances of war, their romance had begun on the home front and their lives together would be lived in the post-war world.

Above left: *Tom and his best man, 1 April 1918. (Cynthia Johnson)*

Above right: *The bridesmaids at Tom and Fanny's wedding, 1 April 1918. (Cynthia Johnson)*

Left: *Fanny and Tom in Pinvin, 1918. (Cynthia Johnson)*

The end at last

Berrow's Worcester Journal noted on 16 November 1918 that: 'In common with other places throughout the Kingdom, Pershore enthusiastically celebrated the news of the signing of the Armistice. The town was full of flags, shops were closed.'

The initial Armistice celebrations, on 11 November 1918, were very much for those on the home front. Of the men and women who had struggled through the conflict, some had suffered the loss or incapacitation of loved ones, others were grateful that their sons, husbands, brothers and lovers would now be returning home. The abbey hosted a service, attended by a number of voluntary organisations, which ended with the Last Post and the National Anthem. After four years of hostilities and hardship it is perhaps not surprising that responses to the end of the fighting expressed a mixture of sadness, relief, exuberance and a touch of jingoism; all of which suggested that it might take a little while to dissipate the animosities stirred up by war.

A GREAT DAY

Monday, November 11th, 1918, was a great day, the greatest in the history of the world for it saw the end of the most terrible war which has ever afflicted humanity. It is with feelings of profound thankfulness that we know that the long struggle has ended in the triumphant victory of Right over Might ...

[We are pleased to note that] there has been little evidence of the disorderly scenes, which disgraced the county on the relief of Mafeking [during the Boer War] nearly twenty years ago. The British people have taken their victory with the same calmness they have maintained throughout the terrible struggle which is now over.

Specific mention was made of the efforts of those on the home front:

The men in the fighting forces, in the army, navy and the air force have the admiration of civilization; but no less wonderful has been the manner of the men and women who have been permitted to remain at home in safety.

Evesham Journal, 16 November 1918

Although the fighting had stopped, the official end of the war was not celebrated until the terms of the peace were negotiated and the Treaty of Versailles was signed on 28 June 1919. At that time, the people of Pershore joined in the country's jubilation:

The news that the peace treaty had been signed was celebrated by the hoisting of the Union Jack on the tower of the Abbey, and ringing of the bells. Mrs Wayne Marriott held a garden party at Avon Bank [where convalescing soldiers had been cared for during the war].

Worcester Herald, 5 July 1919

The Pershore Board of Guardians and the District Council both discussed how best to celebrate the peace, and decided that they would like to buy the grounds around the abbey and create a public recreation park as a memorial. Unfortunately, although the petition was signed by 90 per cent of the town's residents, the proposal was turned down by the landowner.

Nevertheless, the main celebratory activities took place over the August Bank Holiday weekend in 1919, a date that allowed for maximum participation and also coincided with the fifth anniversary of the outbreak of war. By this date, almost all servicemen would have arrived home and begun to take up their former lives.

The keenly anticipated gathering, organised by the Committee of the Pershore and District Old Comrades Association, took place in the fine weather on Tuesday last in the beautiful Abbey Grounds …

Great preparations were made for the reception and entertainment of a big holiday crowd and between 3,000 and 4,000 paid for admission. Of the Old Comrades quite a thousand were invited … and at least 70% of that number from every village and hamlet in the district responded. The nation's emblem floated from the Abbey Church, the town was strikingly beflagged and everybody was in genial mood ready to extend a hearty welcome and recognition to the soldiers which their splendid services deserved.

The Procession was led by the Worcestershire's Regimental Depot Band … Many amusements and side-shows were provided in the grounds including bowling for the pig given by Mr C. Teague of Pershore.

Among the attractions was a tea tent, managed by ladies from Pershore Women's Institute, which attracted many customers on the day.

In the evening the Pershore Town Band played for dancing and the bugle band of the local Cadet Corps, of which the town is justly proud, marched twice round the course. The whole proceedings were reminiscent of the 'good old days' of Pershore's Great Flower Show and all responsible for the organisation are heartily to be congratulated.

Worcester Herald, 9 August 1919

The celebrations also involved sports in which the returned servicemen competed, followed by dinner for them, and a special entertainment for the inmates of the workhouse in the Masonic Hall.

In the years that followed, people had to pick up the pieces and come to terms with their lives. Tom Slaney settled in Birmingham with his new wife, Fanny, and became a clock and watch repairer. Charity continued at home when one of his neighbours initiated a special collection to buy Tom a hand-propelled tricycle so that he could drive himself about. Fanny returned to Pinvin in 1921 when she was expecting her first child. Tom regained the use of his legs following electric shock treatment and hydrotherapy at Droitwich Spa and once again they made their home in Birmingham, regularly visiting Fanny's birthplace in Pinvin.

Peace Day celebration outside Brown's shop. (Marshall Wilson Collection)

Peace Day in Pershore, 16 August 1919. (Marshall Wilson Collection)

Others picked up their lives as best they could. It is worth noting that *Kelly's Commercial Directory* of 1921 lists a number of women still running market gardens on their own, perhaps war widows. After receiving so many incomers in such a short period, the town's population inevitably changed. Although the majority of refugees had returned to Belgium by 1919, some settled in the area and married local residents. Others never had the chance to go home: Henri Sels, a 66-year-old refugee, was billeted in the village of Great Comberton, where he died. He now lies buried in Pershore.

Three years after the hostilities ceased, the townspeople of Pershore gathered in the abbey to see Lord Coventry unveil the new war memorial, upon which was

Tom Slaney retraining to repair clocks and watches. (Cynthia Johnson)

Tom and Fanny with the tricycle in Pinvin. (Cynthia Johnson)

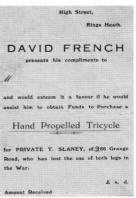

High Street,
Kings Heath.

DAVID FRENCH

presents his compliments to

M

and would esteem it a favour if he would
assist him to obtain Funds to Purchase a

Hand Propelled Tricycle

for PRIVATE T. SLANEY, of 266 Grange
Road, who has lost the use of both legs in
the War.

£ s. d.

Amount Received

GWR 33xx Bulldog class 4-4-0 No. 3353 Pershore Plum at Snow Hill, 1932. (Pershore Heritage Centre)

Fundraising flyer for the tricycle. (Cynthia Johnson)

listed the names of men from the town who were killed in the First World War. At the unveiling, Lord Coventry said people should remember the conflict, and,

> bring their children up in the understanding of what the memorial meant. If the child was a boy, perhaps the call might come in his time and he would do what these men had done. If it was a girl, they should remember the part that women played in the war. The girls should be told what the women of our generation did – how they sent their men to fight and never flinched, however great the sacrifice.
>
> *Berrow's Worcestershire Journal*, 5 November 1921

In Pershore, as in numerous other town and villages across Britain, there were many men and women who had not taken up arms to fight, but who had made a significant contribution nonetheless. Willingly or not, many had sacrificed their sons, brothers and husbands to the frontline in the First World War but the conflict overturned the lives and livelihoods of people on the home front in many other ways. Young or old, locals, refugees, migrants, students, land girls and local women, volunteers, prisoners of war, Boy Scouts and school children had laboured in numerous ways to ensure that both the civilian population and military were provided with an adequate food supply. In acknowledgement of this, in 1927, an aging Bulldog class Great Western Railway locomotive (no. 3353) was renamed the *Pershore Plum* at the request of the Worcester Branch of the National Farmers Union, to commemorate the contribution of the Vale's fruit harvests to wartime food production. For our part, we hope the research and writing of this book, the stories, words and images found will contribute to ensuring that those who fought on the rural home front of World War One are not forgotten.

FURTHER READING

Ambrose, L.M., *A Great Rural Sisterhood: Madge Robertson Watt and the ACWW* (Toronto: University of Toronto Press, 2015).

Andrews, M., *The Acceptable Face of Feminism: The Women's Institute as a Social Movement* (London: Lawrence & Wishart, 1997, reprinted 2015).

Andrews, M., Gregson, A., and Peters, J., *Voices of the First World War: Worcestershire's War* (Stroud: Amberley Publishing, 2014).

Andrews, M. and Lomas, J., *The Home Front in Britain: Images, Myths and Forgotten Experiences since 1914* (Basingstoke: Palgrave Macmillan, 2014).

British Food Policy during the First World War (London: Allen & Unwin, 1985).

Barnett, M., *British Food Policy during the First World War* (Oxford: Routledge 1985 reprinted 2014).

Barrett, P. and Wilson, M., *The Book of Pershore* (Buckingham: Barracuda Books, 1980).

Beckett, I., *Home Front 1914–1918: How Britain Survived the Great War* (Kew: The National Archives, 2006).

Bibbings, L.S., *Telling Tales About Men: Conceptions of Conscientious Objectors to Military Service During the First World War* (Manchester: MUP, 2009).

Bramford, M., *Voices from the Past: Pershore 1900–1935* (Malvern: Aspect Design, 2015).

Braybon, G. and Summerfield, P., *Out of The Cage: Women's Experiences in Two World Wars* (London: Pandora Press, 1987).

Burge, T., *Pershore Men of the Great War 1914–1918* (Greyhound, 2014).

Butcher, G.W., *Allotments for All: The Story of a Great Movement* (London: G. Allen & Unwin, 1918).

Byron, M., *May Byron's Jam Book* (London: Hodder and Stoughton, 1916).

Byron, M. and Pipien, E., *The Great War Cook Book* (Stroud: Amberley Publishing, 2014).

Carney, M., *A Worcestershire Parish at War* (Stroud: Amberley Publishing, 2010).

Charman, T., *The First World War on the Home Front* (London: Andre Deutsch, 2014).

Cooksley, P.G., *Home Front: Civilian Life in World War One* (Stroud: The History Press, 2006).

DeGroot, G., *Back in Blighty: The British at Home in World War One* (London: Vintage, 2014).

Dewey, P.E., *British Agriculture in the First World War* (Oxford: Routledge, 1989, reprinted 2014).

Doyle, P., *First World War Britain: 1914–1919* (Oxford: Shire Publications, 2012).

Duffett, R., *The Stomach for Fighting: Food and the Soldiers of the Great War* (Manchester: MUP, 2012).

Freeman, M., *Pershore Revisited* (Stroud: Tempus, 2005).

Freeman, M., *Pershore Through Time* (Stroud: Amberley Publishing, 2010).

Gaut, R.C., *A History of Worcestershire Agriculture and Rural Evolution* (Worcester: Littlebury Press, 1939).

Ginn, P., Goodman, R. and Langlands, A., *Edwardian Farm: Rural Life at the Turn of the Century* (London: Pavilion, 2010).

Gordon, C., *Coventrys of Croome* (Chichester: Phillimore in association with the National Trust, 2000).

Gosling, L., *Knitting for Tommy: Keeping the Great War Soldier Warm* (Stroud: The History Press, 2014).

Grayzel, S.R., *Women and the First World War* (Harlow: Pearson, 2002).

Gregory, A., *The Last Great War: British Society and the First World War* (Cambridge: Cambridge University Press, 2005).

Hatton Turnor, C., *Our food supply: Perils and Remedies* (London: Country Life, 1916).

Holloway, G., *Women and Work in Britain since 1840* (London: Routledge, 2015)

Howkins, A., *Reshaping Rural England: A Social History 1850–1925* (London: Routledge, 1991).

Howkins, A., *The Death of Rural England: A Social History of the Countryside Since 1900* (London: Routledge, 2003).

Humphries, S. and van Emden, R., *All Quiet on the Home Front: An Oral History of Life in Britain during the First World War* (London: Headline, 2004).

Jones, R., *Worcestershire at Work in Old Photographs* (Stroud: Sutton Publishing Ltd, 1994).

Kushner, T., *Remembering Refugees: Then and Now* (Manchester: MUP, 2006).

Mansfield, N., *English Farmworkers and Local Patriotism, 1900–1930*, (Basingstoke: Ashgate, 2001).

Middleton, T.H., *Food Production in War* (Oxford: The Clarendon Press, 1923).

Oldmeadow, E., *Home cookery in war-time* (London: Grant Richards, 1915).

Pankhurst, E.S., *The Home Front: A Mirror to Life in England during the First World War* (London: Cresset Library, 1987).

Peel, C.S., *The Eat Less Meat War Ration Cookery Book* (London: John Lane; New York: John Lane Co., 1918).

Springhall, J., *Youth, Empire and Society* (London: Croom Helm, 1977).

Stacke, H., *The Worcestershire Regiment in the Great War* (Kidderminster: Cheshire & Sons, 1928).

Strachey, R., *The Cause* (London: Virago, 1928, reprinted 1969).

Watt, Mrs Alfred and Lloyd, N., *The First Women's Institute School* (London: NFWI Publication, 1918).

Williams, D.E., Worcestershire Federation of Women's Institutes, *Madame President, fellow members: The Story of the Worcestershire Federation of Women's Institutes* (Worcester: The Federation, 1980).

Winter, J., *The Great War and the British People* (London: Palgrave Macmillan, 2003).

Women's Co-operative Guild, *Maternity: Letters from Working Women* (1915, reprinted London: Virago, 1978).

Wood, T.B., *The National Food Supply in Peace and War* (Cambridge: University Press, 1917).

INDEX

Abbey 11, 19, 91, 99, 103, 108, 109, 115, 121, 122, 125
Armed forces and army 12, 14, 15, 19, 20, 21, 26, 27, 28-9, 37, 39, 47, 56, 68, 72, 75, 90, 102, 105, 121
Alcohol and public houses 25, 39, 56, 59, 111-3
Allotments 30, 41, 52, 57, 70, 72
Baden Powell, Olave, Robert and Agnes 99, 100, 103
Baskets 16, 31, 33, 36, 45, 98
Belgium and Belgian refugees 21, 24-26, 125
Blackberries 62, 83, 98, 105
Blackout 110, 111
Boy Scouts 15, 20, 43, 44, 98, 99, 100, 101, 126
Boys' Brigade 98, 99, 100-2
Bread 12, 14, 16, 45, 65, 67, 68, 70, 72, 75, 106
Bredon 14, 81, 97, 106
Brickell 91, 92
Cadbury, Mrs Barrow 25
Cadet Corps 100, 102-3, 109, 122
Canning 14, 74, 78, 90, 96
Casualties 26-29, 51
Charity 25, 60, 61, 104, 114-116, 123
Chick, Annie 11, 91
Children 11, 25, 29, 43, 45, 46, 51, 59, 64, 68, 92, 97-109, 114, 117, 125, 126
Christmas 25, 28, 29, 65, 66
Clegg, P.C. 112
Co-operation 41, 42, 87, 86, 87, 89, 94, 100
Co-operative Market 13, 34, 35, 36, 37, 38, 41, 42, 78, 86, 90, 112, 114, 115
Cole, Fanny 116, 117, 118, 119, 120, 123, 124
Communal Kitchen 93
County War Agriculture Committees 39, 41, 47, 49, 57, 81, 87, 90, 94
Croome Park 7, 9, 10, 20, 73, 74, 88, 90, 105, 113, 128
Deerhurst, Viscount 20, 68
Deerhurst Viscountess, 87, 89-90, 92
Defford 23, 24, 27, 30, 34, 93, 102, 106, 112, 113
Earl of Coventry 9, 10, 20, 47, 57,

60, 72, 73, 77, 87, 88, 89, 116, 125, 128
Eggs 63, 66, 96
Elmley Castle 23, 45, 49, 52, 102
Evesham 9, 14, 16, 28, 34, 37, 40, 41, 45, 52, 54, 55, 56, 68, 74, 113, 118
Factory 43, 73, 74, 77, 78, 79
Families 8, 14, 19, 23, 26, 30, 46, 49, 58, 59, 61, 62, 63, 65, 67, 68, 83, 91, 94, 110, 114
Farmers 14, 16, 37, 38, 39, 41, 42, 47, 48, 49, 51, 52, 54, 55, 56, 57, 72, 87, 90, 98, 105, 107, 114, 115, 126
Food 12, 13, 16, 17, 30-42, 51, 56, 57, 58, 62, 65, 66, 67, 68, 70, 71, 72-84, 85, 86, 88, 90, 92, 93, 94, 103, 126, 127, 128
Fruit picking 14, 15, 16, 76, 98, 99, 101, 102, 105
Harvest 5, 15, 20, 25, 38, 39, 40, 43-57, 60, 67, 77, 83, 97, 98, 99, 101, 102, 104
Hooper, Geoffrey Fielder 34, 35, 37, 51, 87, 88, 91, 93
Hooper, Edith 36, 88, 91, 92
Hospital 27, 28, 54, 91, 93, 96, 107, 113
Hudson Captain Warren and Audrey 21, 22, 26, 27
Hynes, Will 49, 50, 51, 52, 111
Jam 5, 14, 15, 16, 30, 66, 67, 69, 70, 72-84, 85, 94, 96, 98, 127
Land Army, land girls and women on the land 15, 39, 44, 45, 48, 49, 51, 52, 53, 56, 57, 87, 126
Lawson Revd F.R. 21, 23
Letters 26, 28, 29, 48, 50, 51, 56, 56, 80, 88, 90, 97, 119, 120
Malvern 14, 42, 84, 99, 105, 107
Market Gardens 19, 30-42, 44, 46, 47, 54, 55, 56, 57, 59, 60, 72, 87, 88, 89, 90, 99, 105, 115, 124
Marrow 55, 84, 114, 115
Masonic Hall 25, 78, 88, 89, 92, 100, 123
Memorial 11, 13, 26, 27, 108, 109, 122, 125
Music hall 20, 21, 22, 113
Peace 19, 86, 109, 113, 121, 122, 123

Peile Archdeacon 23
Pinvin 30, 41, 42, 59, 60, 117, 120, 123, 124
Plum 14, 15, 31, 33, 45, 48, 65, 66, 67, 72, 75, 76, 79, 82, 83, 99, 100, 102, 105, 114, 126
Potatoes 28, 48, 49, 55, 56, 63, 68, 70, 90, 94, 97, 116
POWs 54-57, 115
Pulp and pulping 14, 16, 72, 76, 77, 78, 79, 80, 83, 84
Prices 36, 58, 63, 69, 73, 94
Queues for food 12, 81
Rabbit 62, 63, 93
Rail services and trains 14, 15, 22, 37, 38, 54, 55, 73, 74, 77, 78, 90, 102, 113, 126
Rations and rationing 12, 16, 70, 72, 75, 76
Recipes 63, 65, 66, 69, 70, 72, 73, 93
Recruitment and military tribunals 19-22, 26, 29, 30, 38, 39, 43, 47, 48
Romance 110, 116-20
Salt 82
Schools and schoolchildren 15, 25, 38, 43, 68, 91, 92, 96, 97, 98, 103, 105, 106, 107, 108, 113, 126
Slaney Tom 117, 118, 119, 120, 123, 124
Smallholders 14, 30, 36, 37, 41, 55
Sugar 12, 38, 63, 66, 67, 68, 70, 73, 76, 77, 78, 80, 81, 82, 83, 84, 93
Spiers 31, 32
Tiddesley Woods 14
The Angel 89, 92
Three Tuns public house 110
Tractors and mechanization 40-42
Vegetables 14, 15, 31, 37, 43, 55, 60, 62, 67, 68, 72, 77, 78, 79, 84, 90, 94, 97, 115
Watt, Madge 85, 86, 87, 88, 91, 96,
Wick, 26, 27, 37, 44, 52, 59, 93, 102
Widows 39, 51, 61, 67, 89, 124
Willis, Revd J. 112, 113
Wives 9, 12, 25, 28, 29, 34, 36, 50, 51, 58, 60, 66, 67, 68, 72, 73, 80, 82, 83, 84, 88, 89, 90, 91, 94, 95, 96, 99, 114, 123
Women's Institute 84, 85-96, 122